Praise for *The Whole Spectrum of Social, Motor, and Sensory Games*

"This authentically something-for-everyone book is a joyous reaffirmation that children learn best through fun, imagination, simple materials, and exploration of the many wondrous things of which their bodies and minds are capable. A timely guide the the timeless kind of child's play that should not be allowed to slip into history."

—Ellen Notbohm, author, *Ten Things Every Child with Autism Wishes You Knew*

"Barbara Sher understands children! In her new book, she not only gives great ideas for play, but creatively weaves stories into the book to show how to involve children and excite their attention."

—Kathleen Morris, MS, CCC-SLP creator of *S.I.Focus* magazine and author of *Sensory Soup*

"A resourceful book that takes the 'Power of Play' to the next level."

—Jennifer Gilpin Yacio, editor, *Sensory Focus Magazine*

"A treasure chest of creative ideas for adding play to the learning experience. Not only teachers, but parents, grandparents, and caregivers will welcome this wealth of ideas for engaging children in these playful and educational games that foster skill development, engage reluctant children, and create shared joy and focused excitement."

—Phyllis Booth, author, *Theraplay*

"A book that has a rich variety of play activities that are gentle on the budget and are layered and tailored to appeal to different personalities and developmental abilities."

—Lorna d'Entremont, M.Ed., *Special Needs Book Review*

"What I really found to be encouraging is the variations of those activities, which help to stay fresh."

—Marla Roth-Fisch, award-winning author/illustrator, *Sensitive Sam* and VP, Sensory Processing Disorder Foundation

"Everyone from grandmothers to therapists will benefit from the easy and practical activities in this book. The author's personal anecdotes and video clips are heart-warming and made the book come alive."

—Darlene Mannix, Special Education Teacher and author, *Social Skills Activities for Special Children*

Other books by Barbara Sher

Self-Esteem Games: 300 Fun Activities That Make Children Feel Good About Themselves

Spirit Games: 300 Fun Activities That Bring Children Comfort and Joy

Smart Play: 101 Fun, Easy Games That Enhance Intelligence

Attention Games: 101 Fun, Easy Games That Help Kids Learn to Focus

Early Intervention Games: Fun, Joyful Ways to Develop Social and Motor Skills in Children with Autism Spectrum or Sensory Processing Disorders

The Whole Spectrum of Social, Motor, and Sensory Games

The Whole Spectrum of Social, Motor, and Sensory Games

Using Every Child's Natural Love of
Play to Enhance Key Skills and
Promote Inclusion

BARBARA SHER

WITH

KAREN BEARDSLEY

ILLUSTRATIONS BY RALPH BUTLER

JB JOSSEY-BASS™
A Wiley Brand

Published by Jossey-Bass™
A Wiley Brand
One Montgomery Street, Suite 1200, San Francisco, CA 94104-4594—www.josseybass.com

Jossey-Bass books and products are available through most bookstores. To contact Jossey-Bass directly call our Customer Care Department within the U.S. at 800-956-7739, outside the U.S. at 317-572-3986, or fax 317-572-4002.

Wiley publishes in a variety of print and electronic formats and by print-on-demand. Some material included with standard print versions of this book may not be included in e-books or in print-on-demand. If this book refers to media such as a CD or DVD that is not included in the version you purchased, you may download this material at http://booksupport.wiley.com. For more information about Wiley products, visit www.wiley.com.

Library of Congress Cataloging-in-Publication Data

Sher, Barbara, author.
　　The whole spectrum of social, motor and sensory games : using every child's natural love of play to enhance key skills and promote inclusion / Barbara Sher with Karen Beardsley.
　　　　pages　cm
　　Includes bibliographical references and index.
　　　ISBN 978-1-118-34571-9 (pbk.), ISBN 978-1-118-42014-0 (pdf), ISBN 978-1-118-41669-3 (epub)
　　　　1. Games.　2. Educational games.　3. Child development.　I. Title.
　　GV1203.S4953　2013
　　790.1'922—dc23

2013007721

Printed in the United States of America

FIRST EDITION
PB Printing　　　　10　9　8　7　6　5　4　3　2　1

Contents - - - - - - - - - - - - - - - - -

CHAPTER 2   Games for Babies   47

Daily Games to Play with Babies to Develop the Brain and Deepen the Adult-Child Connection

CHAPTER 3 Progressive Games for Ages Three to Seven   79

Inclusive Games That Use Only One Material to Enhance Multiple Skills

CHAPTER 4 Therapy Games for Ages Three to Twelve 157

Home Therapy Games That Enhance the Basic Skill Domains

CHAPTER 5 Short Group Games for Ages Three to Fifteen   207

Quick Movement Games That Stimulate Thinking, Feeling, and Creativity

For my Dream Team and the many children we have loved at work
For my husband and the many ways he shows love at home
And for my children and grandchildren for everything, always

—Barbara, Mom, and Bubbie

In loving memory of my parents, who took the time to play with me,
and to my daughters, who continue to do so

—Karen and Mom

Preface -

We all know that each child is his or her own unique person with individual interests and skills. We also know that most children go through the same crawl-before-you-can-walk developmental sequences, although some children walk at ten months and others walk at eighteen months. There is a range we all respect. However, all children need experience. Infants are born without a clue about how to move their body; it's the caregiver giving her baby time on his tummy to strengthen his back and putting toys slightly out of reach who helps her baby learn which muscles to use to inch forward. It's the toys that are hung above a baby's crib that help her develop her vision and the skills of reaching and grasping. Being in a playgroup or with others at the park can expose a child to an awareness of facial and body cues.

Experience is always the best teacher, no matter what age we are and what skill we are trying to learn. And for the first five years of life in particular, experience makes all the difference. It has been only in the last ten years that brain researchers have explained how a child's brain develops and grows according to what the child has experienced. We have learned that each time a new activity is consciously experienced, new synapses are formed and the brain enlarges. We have also learned that the one hundred billion neurons that babies are born with and that are connected by practice become atrophied without experiences.

This book is about ways of making these learning experiences fun for children by turning them into games. When children are laughing while they are doing something, they are engaged, and they are learning. When parents and teachers are enjoying the activities as much as their children, or when children are inspired to do the activities on their own, children's skills flourish. You may realize that you already do many of these kinds of activities, but you want to learn more. As you read this book, you will see ways you can use many games to fit your special child. There are games that are perfect for the child on the autism spectrum, whereas others work well for a child who is hyperactive, and almost all can include neurotypical children. Modify or mix and match, and your child's smiling response will let you know if you've picked the games that suit him.

What Key Skills Are Being Enhanced in the Games?

All of these games address motor, sensory, and social skills in one way or another.

The sensory skills include ones that stimulate the five senses, especially vision, hearing, and touch. The tactile system, the largest sensory system in the body, is composed of receptors in the skin that send information to the brain concerning such factors as light touch, pain, temperature, and pressure. The input gives form to body and spatial awareness and plays an important role in enabling an individual to perceive the environment and establish protective reactions for survival.

The motor games work on proprioceptive and vestibular skills. Proprioceptive skills provide us with a subconscious awareness of body position and how the body is moving. They allow us to adjust automatically in different situations, such as stepping off a curb, sitting in a chair, or staying upright on uneven surfaces. Even fine motor tasks, such as writing, using a soup spoon, or buttoning a shirt, depend on an efficient proprioceptive system.

The vestibular system is found in the inner ear and detects movement and changes in the position of the head. It is how we relate in space and know, for example, if we are right side up or tilted to one side. The information we receive from this system tells us which muscles to tighten to keep our balance, and so affects our muscle tone and coordination. All other types of sensation are processed according to vestibular information, so it is a unifying system in our brain.

Social skills include the being aware of others; attending to what is happening in the present moment; and learning to share, take turns, play cooperatively, and read social cues.

The Videos

Some of the games include links to short video clips. These are included to help you see how the games are organized. For visual learners, which many of us are, this type of presentation can make directions instantly easy to understand. These are not professional videos. They were taken in classrooms where I've worked by teachers Marlon Cabrera, Juana Atalig, Patty Staal, and Ivan Garces. I hope these videos will give you a better sense of how simple, fun, engaging, and inclusive these games really are.

The children are from Head Start centers in Saipan and Tinian. Saipan and Tinian are American protectorates in the Commonwealth of Northern Mariana Islands (CNMI). Although I am from Northern California, I work during the school year for the Special Education Department at the three islands in the CNMI: Saipan, Rota, and Tinian. As an occupational therapist wanting to increase the motor, social, and sensory skills of children with special needs, I go into each child's classroom and present games for all the children that target the skills I want "my" child to learn. In this way, the child with special needs also gets the benefit of feeling part of the group.

In the videos, I do not identify which child has special needs because the point of seeing the games is to notice how everyone can use practice in all the skills and how much fun all the children are having by playing the games together.

How the Book Is Organized

The first chapter presents spontaneous games for all ages, because sometimes an improvised moment can be the best teaching. In addition to enhancing skills, these games can make waiting at the doctor's office or for food at a restaurant enjoyable, helping raise spirits and put everyone in a good mood. "Whose Hand Is on Top?" for example, is a great family game in which everyone has silly fun together but all have to pay attention to keep track of whose hand moves next. And "Ways to Walk" is ideal if you've got a cranky kid not happy about walking a distance. If everyone takes gigantic giant steps and mincing baby steps to get there, you will end up with children who are in a much better mood.

The second chapter includes lots of fun games you would do one-on-one with your little one. They work in particular on the foundational sensory and motor skills on which all other skills are built. As with other games in this book, you only need to look around the house to find the materials you need to engage and lengthen your baby's attention.

The third chapter is full of progressive games. Progressive games continually change to challenge different skills, but each series of games can be done with just one easy-to-find material. For example, kids can start by jumping over a rope that is slowly raised, requiring increasing strength to jump over it. This same rope can then be slowly lowered so that children have to continually adjust their posture to go under it without touching it. The rope can even be wiggled so children have to manage their timing to make it over without the wiggly rope touching them, and so on. Most of the links to videos are in this chapter so that you can access visual information on how to play each set of games. These games can be played in the inclusive classroom or with any mixed group of young children, such as siblings and neighbors.

Chapter Four, written by occupational therapist Karen Beardsley, provides therapy games for a wide range of children from ages three to twelve. Karen is very experienced and knowledgeable and has that same let-it-be-fun spirit. Her games include ones played in small spaces, such as "Flipping Pancakes," and others that are played outdoors, such as "Flying Meteorite." The games are organized by type of skill you want to focus on. Karen also contributed the appendix for home therapists and parents who are thinking of inviting a home therapist to work with their child.

The fifth chapter presents group games for children ages three to fifteen. Each game has a single theme, and there is a large range of games to accommodate the different interests of the various ages. An example of a game for little ones is stacking cans in "Can You Do the Can-Can," whereas older children enjoy "Bowling for Dollars." One group game has older kids making up a cool group dance, and another has preschoolers jumping on letters.

The Stories

Scattered throughout are personal stories that tell of experiences I have had with children I work with, as well as my own children and grandchildren. My hope is to give you a sense of who I am, to show you real ways that games can fit into daily life, and to amuse you with tales of the joys and frustrations of being with children.

Acknowledgments ·-·-·-·-·-·-·-·-·-·-·

Barbara's

My guiding plan when working with children in a classroom is to include everyone. To that aim, I use games in which there is room for children of differing skills to play together. These are games that can also be played at home and in neighborhoods where children of varying ages and abilities play together. To see which games work best, I needed playful teachers, aides, and parents and, most important, scores of children!

I am so appreciative of all the children at all the Head Start centers who played with me and would enthusiastically greet me when I came in the door, *knowing that a game was coming.* Big love also goes to their teachers, who were and are enthusiastic about my bringing games into their classroom, especially Quin Besong, Miranda Smith, Juana Atalig, and Ivan Garces, the amazing impresario for our shows.

It may take a village to raise a child, but it also takes a dedicated team to make a difference in the life of a child with special needs. I work with such a team. They are a group of fine people who know how to laugh and play and care. There is an expression that goes, "If you've seen a child with autism, you've seen a child with autism," meaning that like all children, each child with autism has his or her own unique interests, skills, strengths, and needs. One size does not fit all. One way of working with children is not "the" way.

I'm grateful to our Dream Team, who understand this and work toward knowing each child well. They are the special education teachers and the related service staff in the Early Childhood Department of the Northern Mariana Islands Public School System: Leilani Nielsen, Mary-Margaret Peyton, Yoli and Chrislaine Lely, Rose and Jerry Diaz, Joe Cruz, Jacob Villagomez, Mark and Patty Staal, and Mercy Tisa and Marlon Cabrera—the last of whom captured most of the great video shots of kids playing the Progressive Games and Short Group Games.

We are also fortunate to have a director with vision, Suzanne Lizama, who is willing to grow and be open to ever better possibilities in working with and evaluating the whole child.

Writing a book is also a collaborative effort. It starts with an idea and expands to many other people. I am thrilled that my former colleague and dear friend Karen Beardsley, whose work I have always admired, agreed to enrich this book with her home therapy ideas.

I've always admired my editor, Kate Bradford, for her diligent and careful editing, but now I am also enjoying getting to know her good sense of humor. Thanks also to copyeditor Francie Jones, who added her thorough editing skills. Ralph Butler never fails to come up with a joyful group of people in his illustrations, and I appreciate his willingness to match my visions. I must mention Nana Twumasi and Justin Frahm, Wiley associates who are fast to answer whatever questions I have and contribute their valuable touch. My thank-yous to them all, and to the others who are part of the production group whom I have never met, but who are, I know, of great importance to the final product.

Gratitude extends beyond the writing of this book. It belongs to the people in my life, such as my sisters, Bonnie Wilson, Trisha Ferlic, and Glo Harris, who have always cheered me on. Two people, however, get special recognition. One is my nephew Marc Wilson, who taught me how to love my iMovie feature. The other is my dear brother, Monty Sher, who expresses his understanding of the synergy of my games with his articulate words.

And—as if it were even possible to have a good life without close women friends—I owe so much to my wonderful Saipan buddies, Rita Bonnici, Susan Baetge, Jenny Slack, Patty Staal, Mary Peyton, and Jill Derickson, for all the lovely and meaningful walks and talks; to Janet McCulloch for so many insightful conversations; and to my dear Humboldt lifelong, loving friends, Lorraine Carolan, Cindy Taylor, and Joan Becker.

I also want to give recognition to two people who are an enormous help in my life, Lorna Arcega and Mario Santillan.

As always and forever, I depend on the support and continuous love of my own wonderful, talented, beautiful, and intelligent daughters, Roxanne and Marissa, and my adorable and bright grandchildren, Oliver and Julien. I also have the good fortune to have spectacular sons-in-law, Ehren and Mark, who have always been so good to me.

And I'm grateful to the universe for bringing this former widow a warm, funny, kind, loving, and handsome husband, Don Cohen, who is my comfortable ballast, cuddly companion, and head cook. He makes our life work smoothly in our tree house home by the sea.

My love and gratitude for you all.

Karen's

We learn through play, and should never underestimate its power. A dear friend and fellow colleague of mine once told me, "I see myself kind of like an inspirational fairy, sprinkling permission for therapists, teachers, and parents to make fun use of whatever they have, to do therapy with." Her name is Barbara Sher, and I am grateful for her invitation to collaborate on this wonderful project. I hope we have been able to accomplish a bit of this inspirational work with this book and our games.

To the children around the world, thank you for teaching me to be the therapist I am.

To the parents of these children, thank you for welcoming me into your homes and lives.

To the professionals with whom I have worked, thank you for your wisdom when I needed guidance.

To my husband, Don, thank you for your support and eternal confidence in me.

To my two beautiful and loving daughters, Kaya and Raina, thank you for inspiring me with your creativity, your eagerness to always play with me, and your honest critiques of my games. But mostly, thank you for teaching me that the importance of most anything we do in life all starts in the home.

The Whole Spectrum of Social, Motor, and Sensory Games

Introduction - ᵕ ᵕ ᵕ ᵕ ᵕ ᵕ ᵕ ᵕ ᵕ ᵕ ᵕ ᵕ

The Power of Play and the Synergy of Games

This book is about play. As such, it confronts a common prejudice: play is frivolity, incidental to life's purposes and direction. Right? No. Of course there are contexts in which play is frivolity for its own sake—but at the foundation of what makes us human, play is central. This is true for all of us, but particularly true for the developmentally atypical. Still, let's briefly examine the importance of play for all of us.

To quote Stuart Brown, psychiatrist, scientist, clinical researcher, and founder of the National Institute for Play, "Neuroscientists, developmental biologists, psychologists, social scientists, and researchers from every point of the scientific compass now know that play is a profound biological process. It shapes the brain."[1]

This is true for all children. Stanley Greenspan, author and noted authority on children with autism spectrum disorder, emphasized the importance of the "floortime" approach: getting down and creatively playing on the floor with these children can make a significant difference in their brain growth and subsequent increases in skills.[2]

The instant effect of joyful play on brain growth was shown dramatically when two groups of typical children had brain imaging done before and after activities. One group's activities were watching TV, playing repetitive video games, and the like. The other kids were engaged in activities that were exciting for them, such as playing with a train and making up stories about the action taking place. The brain images from the children not particularly engaged showed no changes. But the brain images from the children who were playfully engaged in these multisensory creative activities showed immediate differences. New synaptic connections were actually visible in the brain scans![3]

In brain-speak, stimulating experiences activate certain neural synapses, and this triggers growth processes that consolidate those connections. Rich experiences, in other words, really do produce rich brains.

Abundant scientific research, such as that conducted by Marian Diamond at UC Berkeley in the 1960s, shows that even rats placed in an enriched environment with opportunities to play with others will thrive. The more a young rat plays, the more rapidly its brain grows.

Play makes us smarter. But there is more.
Peter Gray, a specialist in developmental and evolutionary psychology, adds to this idea of play making us human. In a series of essays, Gray observes that play occurs among the young of many species and seems clearly to promote skill learning and practice. It has been observed that playfulness among primates serves as a means of defeating aggression and mitigating dominance. As Gray says, "We inherited these play-enabling signals and restraints from our primate ancestors, and then—through both culture and biological evolution—we built upon them."[4]

Robert Fagen, an animal play behaviorist, explains, "Play allows 'pretend rehearsal' for the challenges and ambiguities of life, a rehearsal in which life and death are not at stake."[5] Play researchers Sergio and Vivian Pellis of the Canadian Centre for Behavioral Neuroscience at the University of Lethbridge (Alberta, Canada) corroborate the notion that play is practice in their book *The Playful Brain*. This erudite book synthesizes decades of research on animal play, showing that play is clearly integral to development—and competence—and that the skills gained through play in navigating social ambiguity are key.[6]

What happens if we don't play?
Brown spells it out in his book *Play*. When social mammals seriously miss out on play, they show similar characteristics: they don't have the ability to

delineate friend from foe; they miss social signaling and either act aggressively or retreat when meeting others; they don't learn the give-and-take of mock combat (taunting from teasing); they can't perceive others' emotional states and adopt an appropriate response; and they have difficulty connecting emotionally with others.

Is this true for all social mammals, namely, us?

Darell Hammond is the inspiration behind KaBOOM!, the world-class nonprofit that has harnessed the power of community to build and renovate, so far, over two thousand playgrounds. As Hammond points out on his Web page, "The Play Deficit is the very real decline in play in our society. Children are playing less than any previous generation. . . . Play is the primary means by which children develop, and lack of play is causing them profound physical, intellectual, social, and emotional harm. . . . During play, children learn to work in groups, share, negotiate, resolve conflicts, and act for themselves. Children who do not play are at an increased risk for displaying problems during more formalized social interactions. . . . If play is not made a priority, we will continue to see a decrease in creativity and imagination, as well as vital skills including curiosity, social skills, resiliency, and the ability to assess risk."[7]

Play, then, allows us to be more socially approachable and open to learning, creating better social interactions with other people.

How do you intertwine play with these children's lives?

Introducing play activities, examples of which you will see in this book, into these children's lives reopens their social world. Of course, this entry must be managed deliberately and with care. Playing with typical peers is integral to the experience, as is play with a loving caretaker. As you will see, some of the play activities seem to border on the simplistic. Yet it is their very simplicity that makes them accessible and acceptable to the child with special needs. You will see children's delight as they awaken to their new social life. As this life unfolds, they can explore the freedom and equality in the play state, interacting with some safety from being dominated or controlled by others. They begin to learn what it means to be in tune with others. Indeed, literally sharing musical tunes with others is an important part of this process.

You will find a rich variety of play activities in this book. There may be a temptation to see them as isolated, unconnected activities. That would be a mistake. Every activity is layered. Every activity combines a variety of modalities: movement, touching, looking, interacting, and so on. Every sense is engaged. There is evolution from the simple skills to the more complex.

Finally, it is important to recognize that these play activities are synergistically potent. That phrase is a mouthful, but it contains a truth. All these play activities interact in ways that enhance each other, making the learning richer. The resulting achievements become the foundation for still further achievement.

But the best part of all these ideas is this: when we play games with children, we can all have fun.

Notes

1. Brown, S., and Vaughan, C., *Play: How It Shapes the Brain, Opens the Imagination, and Invigorates the Soul*, New York: Avery, 2009.

2. Greenspan, S., and Wiede, S., *Engaging Autism: Using the Floortime Approach to Help Children Relate, Communicate, and Think*, New York: Da Capo, 2009.

3. Begley, S., "Your Child's Brain," *Newsweek*, v127 n8 February 18, 1996, http://www.thedailybeast.com/newsweek/1996/02/18/your-child-s-brain.html

4. Gray, P., *Psychology* (4th edition), New York: Worth, 2001.

5. Fagen, R., *Animal Play Behavior*, New York: Oxford University Press, 1981.

6. Pellis, S., and Pellis, V., *The Playful Brain: Venturing to the Limits of Neuroscience*, London: Oneworld, 2010.

7. Hammond, D., KaBOOM!, Washington DC, http://kaboom.org/docs/documents/pdf/Play-Deficit.pdf

We don't stop playing because we grow old; we grow old because we stop playing.

—*George Bernard Shaw*

CHAPTER ONE

Spontaneous Games for All Ages

Children are awake around 12 hours a day, more or less. That's 84 hours a week or 4,368 hours a year that their brains are open and available for learning—and parents are a child's best teacher. However, we caregivers are busy 5,000 hours a year with the demands of work, children, and home. Having to play a game with our child can feel like a lot to ask, even when we know it matters.

One solution is spontaneous games. Games can teach, and they also can change the mood. When our child is a baby, we learn that distraction works. Our child is fussy, and we reach in our pocket and pull out our keys or anything novel to play with and voilà, the child is content and busy.

Preschool kids can be distracted too. For example, I played "Can You Do What I Do? Can You Say What I Say?" with my twin five-year-old grandsons when they were hot and grouchy. They took a moment to warm to the idea, but they got into it and had silly fun coming up with their own variations. Hot and grouchy changed into light and fun. Emotional alchemy!

There are lots of games in this chapter that take a short amount of time and can provide the perfect distraction from a potentially hard moment, such as when standing in a long line, waiting for food to be served at a restaurant, or walking a long distance to get back to the car or bus—or even when children are cleaning their room. There are also silly games to start off the day with a giggle.

The best part of spontaneous games is that they require no materials, or only what is probably lying around. The even better part is that they give parents easy teachable moments, and give children real experience in practicing skills.

Waiting Games for Airports, Restaurants, and Doctor's Offices

Waiting is not easy. Whether waiting for our turn in the dentist's chair or in the grocery line, waiting can bring up angst. As adults, we can get caught up in unhelpful thoughts, such as *I picked the wrong line (again!)—that one is faster!* Young kids might not entertain themselves with these annoying thoughts, they just want to leave! And they can't. So at this point, to keep us all sane, we can bring in the clowns, as it were, and come up with a game.

What Would Mary Poppins Do?

I wanted to be more like Mary Poppins. Instead of screeching at my children, like the Wicked Witch of the West, to clean up yet another big mess they'd made, I wanted to burst into song and, with that "spoonful of sugar," watch the work get done.

I wanted to be Poppins-esque not only because it would make me feel better about my mothering but also because I know how important play is. As a pediatric occupational therapist, I know that fun makes everything go down more easily, and that fun play is how children learn.

So, over the years, I have devised some games that I have used with my own and other children to make the things we have to do more enjoyable. I don't use games every time, but whenever I do, a potentially bad moment is turned into a fun one.

Play and humor and laughter release a hormonal natural high. It's organic, it's free, and it's an all-natural joy jumper—and best of all, it gets the job done.

I came up with this lighthearted way of clearing up a mess when I'd returned from an out-of-town workshop. My young daughters had been left in the company of their loving but not particularly tidy father. I came home to two very happy, healthy girls, but to get to them I had to wade through five days of strewn clothes, game pieces, stale slices of toast, and other flotsam and jetsam. I was delighted to be home, and, fresh from a workshop on singing games for children, I wanted to keep my good mood, practice what I'd learned—and get this overwhelming cleaning job done.

I decided to throw everything, regardless of what it was, into one big pile in the middle of the room, and then sort it all out. To the tune of "The Bear Went over the Mountain," I began tossing everything into the pile while singing:

> Put everything in a pi-ile
> Put everything in a pi-ile
> Put everything in a pi-IIIILE
> In the middle of the room!
> The middle of the room
> The middle of the room
> Put everything in a pi-IIIILE
> In the middle of the room

My then five-year-old was immediately suspicious that this might be work, but I reminded her that it had to get done no matter what, so we might as well have some fun. She understood, and she and her sister and I tossed everything that was out of place onto the pile, singing and giggling as we made long shots and high tosses. The rooms were quickly cleared of debris, except for the big mound in the middle of the living room. We sat around it as if it were a campfire. I held up each item and, in rhythmic singsong, said, "A sock, a sock, where does it go?" Someone would answer, "The laundry basket!" We did this for each item, and soon the big pile had been separated into smaller piles of books, blankets, laundry, toys, and so on. Everyone was then assigned some piles to put away while I swept the floor. (If you try this game, you can organize the "putting away" aspect according to your child's skill level. A mobile child who can sort will be able to put objects in the correct drawer or shelf. Another child who is not easily mobile might need to have the toy basket put near her chair, with her job being to toss the toys in the basket.) Within a relatively short time, the house was habitable again and we were all still in a good mood.

We used this method often, whenever my daughters' bedrooms—or mine—got in that state of overwhelming messiness. At those times we piled everything on the bed so that the floor and all other areas were clear. Once that was done, the project felt doable—only one pile on the bed needed sorting, instead of the entire room.

I didn't have a song for this bed-piling work, but having an uncluttered house again and all of us helping in our own way sure made me feel like singing.

Game 1: Guess the Winning Number

Waiting for someone to arrive, whether that person is coming in a car to pick you up or getting off the plane, can be anxiety provoking or just plain boring. In this game, you can turn such a moment into a fun contest of who guesses the right number.

Whoever is right gets the satisfaction of being right, while everyone gets the fun of focused attention and counting together in sync, and the relief of being distracted from waiting.

GOALS

Learning to calm anxiety
Diverting attention

DIRECTIONS

You and your child or children each make a guess as to how many cars will pass before the right one stops, or how many people will get off the plane or come down to the baggage claim until the right one arrives. Everyone who has made a guess watches and counts, each hoping that he or she has the winning number.

VARIATION

If everyone's number has passed and still the car or person hasn't shown, no problem: just make new guesses ("It wasn't the sixth car, so now I'm guessing it's the fifteenth").

Game 2: Toothpick Art

GOALS

Creativity
Fine motor skills

MATERIALS

A few toothpicks (often available at restaurants)

DIRECTIONS

Make designs together or for each other with toothpicks.

VARIATIONS

1. You can make specific things, such as shapes, squares, rectangles, triangles, and so on, or letters that work well with straight lines, such as *E* and *F* and *M*.

2. You can also just make a design. Cooperative designs are fun, with each person in turn adding a toothpick to make an interesting pattern or until the food finally arrives!

Game 3: Penny Flick

GOALS

Following rules
Fine motor skills

MATERIALS

Pennies or other coins and a table

SETUP

Give each player at the table a penny with the flat side on the table.

DIRECTIONS

Each person moves the penny along the table by flicking with an index finger and thumb or pushing it with just an index finger or the side of the thumb. The method doesn't matter.

VARIATIONS

1. Partners sitting across from each other flick their pennies toward each other. The goal is to see if they can get their pennies to meet and collide in the middle.

2. If more than two want to play together, have all the players flick their pennies into the center of the table and try to get the pennies to bump into each other or hit a specified object, such as the saltshaker. If more than three players, players could form teams of two.

3. Set up two objects, such two cups or just two other pennies, a short distance away from the penny flickers as "goal posts." The players have to flick their pennies between the two objects. Keep making the goal posts closer together to increase the challenge.

4. Using a straw or spoon handle for a hockey stick, call the penny a "puck" and bat the puck back and forth between the players.

5. Make a line of pennies with at least an inch of space between them and have a player try to flick his penny through each of the spaces. Or have the player try to hit each penny and knock it out of line.

Game 4: Which Cup Is It Under?

A classic carnival trick is to capture someone's attention (and make money). Use this tried-and-true method by hiding a coin under a cup. If the player guesses which cup it's under, the money is hers!

GOALS

Focusing
Paying close attention

MATERIALS

Three cups and a coin

SETUP

Place the three cups upside down on the table.

DIRECTIONS

Ask youra child (or children) to look away, and hide a coin under one of the cups—or do it in full view of the child (depending on age and skill). Then move the cups around quickly so it's not clear where the coin is hidden.

If there is more one child playing, have them take turns guessing.

VARIATIONS

1. Use more than three cups to enlarge choices, or only two to reduce choices.
2. Let the child have a turn being the "carnival barker," and you have to guess.
3. For the young child or new learner, use different colored cups—the child has to notice if the coin is under, say, the red cup or the blue cup.

Game 5: Whose Hand Is on Top?

GOALS

Following directions
Timing
Physically interacting with others

SETUP

Sit at a table close enough so you and the child can touch hands.

DIRECTIONS

Put your hand on the table and ask your child to put one of her hands on top of yours. Then put your other hand on top of her hand and ask her to put her other hand on the top of the hand pile. Then you pull your first hand out from under the pile of hands and put it back on top. Encourage her to do the same her hand that is now on the bottom. Keep repeating this pattern, with the hand on the bottom of the pile moving to the top. Start very slowly at first until she gets the idea, and then begin to speed up the action.

VARIATION

Got three or more pairs of hands wanting to play? Silliness ahead!

Game 6: Feely Games

GOALS

Interpreting tactile information
Social interaction

MATERIALS

Small objects that are safe to touch

SETUP

Have the objects ready in your purse or pocket.

DIRECTIONS

The child has to guess without peeking and only feeling what is in your purse or coat pocket. Tell your child to close her eyes and reach into your purse or pocket, take out something, and guess what it is without looking. Keep playing until you run out of things, or, if appropriate, let your child find things in the room for you to touch and guess!

VARIATION

If you run out of objects, change it to a seeing texture game, such as I Spy, and take turns having the other player guess what you are looking at with only clues. Clues can work on different concepts, such as color or category as well as texture. For example, "I see something soft and red" (pillow) or "I see something hard that is used for eating" (spoon).

Game 7: Making a Wiggly Worm

GOALS

Focusing
Experimenting

MATERIALS

A wrapped straw and a glass of water

DIRECTIONS

You can turn a straw wrapper into a surprising creature. Get a straw, and instead of pulling off the paper cover, squish it off so that it forms accordion pleats.

Then, put the straw into a glass of water. Put your finger on the top of the straw so it traps a little water in it. Hold the straw over the squished straw wrapper and pick up your finger so a few drops fall from the straw onto the wrapper. The wrapper will almost magically move like a wiggly worm. After you have demonstrated, let the child try doing it himself. She will discover by experimenting that a little water makes the worm move, and too much water drowns it. This discovery will make her more aware of how much water he is trapping and what to do to get more or less water in the straw (also good for another ten minutes of quiet).

VARIATION

If you find you're starting to feel guilty because your child is overly enthusiastic about this game and using too many of the restaurant's straws, change the activity. See if your child can take water from one glass and fill up another using his newly learned straw-filling skill.

Clarifying Judge

It is often very difficult to see things from another's point of view—and for children the task is even more difficult, so egocentric is their viewpoint. When two children are fighting over the same toy, the other person's viewpoint is not even considered.

As caregivers and teachers, we are often called on to be judges. In this lofty position, we can use the dictatorial approach ("Becky, give Laurel the doll this instant") or the laissez-faire approach ("It's your problem. You work it out"). Either way can work . . . sometimes. But sometimes it's time for the "Clarifying Judge." A Clarifying Judge explains to both injured parties what exactly is going on with each of them.

A case in point happened between the then four-year-old Roxanne and her slightly older cousin, Mario. Hearing some screams and cries, I walked into the room and found a tearful Roxanne, who protested that Mario had grabbed a whistle right out of her hand. Mario was quick to defend his actions by explaining that he'd had the whistle first and had only put it down for a second when Roxanne took it and wouldn't give it back. He had to grab it.

I listened thoughtfully to both sides, having not the slightest idea as to who was right or wrong. I decided instead to play it back for them.

"My, this is a problem," I began, "let's see if I understand. Mario, you had the whistle first and weren't done playing with it, but you put it down for a second when Roxanne picked it up. You felt like it was still your turn and asked her for it back, but she wouldn't give it to you, so you got angry and took it." Mario nodded his head slowly, obviously feeling pity for the abused boy I had described.

Roxanne began to protest, and I gestured for her to wait. "Roxanne," I continued, "you had been waiting for your turn with the whistle, and when you saw Mario lay it down, you figured your turn had come. And then when he wanted it back after you'd had it for just a second or so, you felt it was unfair. It seemed like he was getting two turns in a row and you had none. Right?"

Roxanne nodded her head and cast a quick look at Mario.

"What a problem," I continued to empathize. "There is only one whistle, and you both want it. If only there were some way you both could be happy."

I stopped talking and pretended to be lost in thought pondering this weighty problem.

Then Mario, who always was a sweet kid, said earnestly, "I know what. Roxanne could go ahead and have her turn and then give it to me." And he placed the whistle beside Roxanne. Roxanne, who has her moments, turned her back and said in that singsongy voice children sometimes use, "Well now I don't want it." But after a moment's pause, she slyly smiled, pick up the whistle, blew a few notes, and then handed it to Mario. "It's your turn," she said. They smiled at each other.

Sometimes it helps to have a Clarifying Judge.

Game 8: Art for Two

GOALS

Creativity

Fine motor skills

MATERIALS

Paper and pencils, markers, or crayons

DIRECTIONS

Draw a picture together. One person starts off making a shape on paper, any shape. The other player then adds a line or any mark he wants. There is no right or wrong, just continue to take turns creating a design until you both decide you are done. Even if you have zero drawing skills, as long as you are willing to do whatever you can, your child learns that it's okay to start from whatever level he is at.

VARIATIONS

1. With a slightly older child, experiment with drawing people or scenes. Start by drawing a person together. You draw a circle for the head and ask your co-artist to add a body. You add arms, he adds legs, you add fingers, he adds toes, and so on. You can get lots of details in there when you add clothes. Do they have polka dots? Stripes? What is the background? Is there a tree? A house? The sun?

2. You could play this game with more than two people.

Game 9: Secret Writing

Writing invisible letters on a child's back or palm is a fun way to convey a secret message and requires connecting the sense of touch with cognition.

GOALS

Attention
Letter recognition
Tactile awareness

DIRECTIONS

Using your finger, "draw" a letter on your child's back or palm. Keep writing, letter by letter, until you've written a whole message. Take turns so you both get to experience what it feels like.

VARIATIONS

1. If you write on the child's back, have him, at the same time, draw on paper what he thinks is being drawn on his back.

2. For an older child, write words, one letter at a time. For a younger child, do single shapes, numbers, or letters. Have an older child play this game with a younger sibling as a fun way to help him learn his letters and grow his brain.

Game 10: Can You Do What I Do?
Can You Say What I Say?

GOALS

Imitation
Coordination
Creativity

SETUP

Sit facing each other. If there are more than two players, sit in view of each other.

DIRECTIONS

Start this game with the words, "Can you do what I do? Can you say what I say?" (Repeat until you have everyone's attention.) Say it in a singsongy voice and clap your thighs or hands to add emphasis and rhythm. This introduction gets everyone ready to play.

Then do one hand movement accompanied by a sound and have them imitate you. What movement you do depends on the age of the children, but silly is almost always good, such as darting your tongue in and out like a snake while making a humming sound or whatever tickles your fancy. After everyone has done the movement-sound combination for a rhythmic amount, such as five times, you return to the original chant, "Can you do what I do? Can you say what I say?" while doing another movement and sound. You can stay the leader in this, but it's fun to take turns and see what everyone comes up with.

VARIATION

If you are playing this game at home, you aren't limited to stationary movements. If it feels right, stand up and do large muscle moves, such as jumping, and do a 180-degree turn too—or any judo or dance move.

Who Are We Today?

It's not always easy to get children to want to go for a walk, even if it's a beautiful day.

One Saturday morning, I was trying to convince my daughters to take a walk with me. They preferred watching Saturday morning cartoons. Because I was going to walk the paths in the woods behind our house, I tried this ploy: "I'm going to start walking, and when you're ready, see if you can find me." Children perk up when there is a challenge involved.

Because my daughters knew our woods, I took a fork on the path that they knew about but wasn't my usual walk. I wanted to increase the challenge. After a short while, I began to hear some odd sounds behind me and was soon delighted to see that they not only had found me but also had dressed up like Native American scouts looking for me. When they caught up with me, they danced in a circle around me, hooping, hollering, and chanting. I was thrilled.

From that experience, I learned that having a theme will sometimes be the ticket to get kids to walk with me, whether they are grandchildren, neighbor children, or children with special needs.

Possible themes are as follows:

- Shall we be Explorers going down a new street or path and see what we see?
- Shall we be Spies on the lookout for something special, like lost pennies?

- ◆ Shall we be Royalty and inspect the neighborhood to see if everything meets with our approval?
- ◆ Shall we be Birders and see how many birds we can see?

The possibilities are endless.

Maybe the real reason for the game is to get the kids out and moving, because we know that matters for their physical and mental health. But by adding pretend play, we are also encouraging imagination, creativity, and, best of all, a sense that we are adventure-mates together! Let the good times begin.

Walking Outside Games

Walking is a lovely way to spend time together. But sometimes you find your walking partner does not want to enjoy the moment. He complains about being hungry or tired or bored, and yet you still have a ways to go before you get home or back to the car. You need a game!

Game 1: How Many Ways to Walk?

GOALS

Coordination
Imagination
Imitation
Moving in sync

DIRECTIONS

Rather than walk like a regular person, move like someone or something else, such as a giant, mouse, or kangaroo.

VARIATION

Choreograph a movement, such as a repeated pattern—three jumps, ten gallops, and so on. Keep adding different ways to move, such as sliding sideways, walking backward, hopping, jumping, and leaping. Or just hold hands and skip!

Game 2: Stop and Go

GOALS

Motor control
Rhythm
Attention

DIRECTIONS

As you are walking, whether with one child or many, explain that you will suddenly say "Stop!" and everyone, including you, should stop instantly as if frozen (if necessary, show them an example of what "stop" looks like). Then you will say "Go," and everyone should go forward. They won't know when you will suddenly say "Stop" again because you will do it irregularly. Sometimes there will be a long walk between stops, sometimes it will happen almost right away. The fun, for the children, is not knowing when it will come. The fun for you is knowing that you are painlessly getting to where you want to go.

VARIATION

Alternate walking with a big stride (giant steps) or with a little shuffle (baby steps), or combine them. You can decide ahead of time how many steps to take, such as ten giant steps and then ten baby steps, and then repeat that pattern.

Game 3: Glued Together

GOAL

Motor control
Being in sync with another

DIRECTIONS

Pretend you are putting imaginary glue on the child's back and your front—so you are stuck together. Place your hands on your child's shoulders to give you control. Then walk forward, and he walks with you. You can go quite a way with this one.

VARIATION

Try being glued just on your hips for older kids so that you are both facing forward and walking as if one person.

Game 4: Guess the Number of Steps

GOALS

Estimating
Getting the thrill of guessing correctly
Learning from wrong guesses

DIRECTIONS

Guess the number of steps you will take to the next corner, signpost, traffic light, or tree. How far ahead depends on the age of the child. See who was closer to the correct number.

VARIATION

Guess how many seconds or minutes it takes to go to the next spot.

Game 5: Whose Head Is in the Clouds?

Once you have reached your destination, it's time to chill and play this game.

GOALS

Shared attention
Creativity
Imagination

MATERIALS

A sky with a few puffy clouds

DIRECTIONS

This is like I Spy, except players spy different creatures in the clouds and others see if they can see them too. Point out the different parts so all can see the creature (for example, "That trailing part is the tail").

VARIATION

Make up a story about the cloud creatures and what they are doing up there together!

The Benefits of Pretend Play

Playing house and all its variations, like playing store and playing school, are games children take to like ducks to water. There is nothing like a good game of pretend to get everyone in a pleasant mood, me included.

In the game of "house," I like to take the baby role and let them be the parents. There is something about lying back saying, "Goo goo, I want water," and having them scurry around waiting on me that is very satisfying. I sometimes suspect that they tried to set a good example because when I got very unreasonable (I had their other examples to imitate) and said things like "I want my covers on; no, I want them off. I want water. No, yuck, not *that* cup," they patiently complied with each request, cooing softly and gently until they finally outlasted me.

I also liked playing the role of the family dog, Doggy Daisy. Dogs lie around a lot.

When things get chaotic or irritations are on the rise, I strongly suggest giving everyone a break from reality and saying, "Let's play pretend!" Then, come up with a scenario that might entice your child. Once you begin playing, try and stay in character and talk and act the way you imagine the person or animal you are pretending to be would.

"Let's pretend that you are a magical wizard and can transform things, and I will be your assistant." Then follow the child's imagination. Maybe he'll want to change the couch into an elephant, and you can both pretend to be riding it.

"Let's pretend that you are a movie star and I am your makeup person." Then have fun with a bunch of makeup, being appropriately obsequious and fawning.

"Let's pretend that you are Batman and I am Robin, and we can go for a ride in our special-equipped Batmobile looking for crime. What kinds of gadgets would our car have?"

There are so many variations to play. When a child gets a minor scrape, it's a great time to pretend to be a doctor and rush her to the "hospital" (which is your couch). Lay her down and do all sorts of doctor-like things with your imaginary stethoscope and tongue depressor. Use real medicated salve and bandages, if needed or even if not needed. Kids will, I've noticed, be far better patients when I pretend I am a "doctor tending to their 'boo-boos.'" I guess it must be something about having more confidence in a professional.

When you are serving dinner, pretend sometime that the room is a fancy restaurant and you are a snotty waiter. Even more fun for me was to pretend I was Thelma from Sloppy Joe's eatery—"Don't be asking for anything not on the menu." My kids didn't try that with Thelma. They knew that with her you can "like it or lump it."

Imagination is the key to creativity. Pretending is a safe way to try out ideas. It also gives children the opportunity to try on different personas and different attitudes and understand the nuances of different personalities. Better than learning how to "read social cues" is to try them on yourself!

Games Just for Little Ones (Ages Two to Seven)

Game 1: A, You're Adorable

When my children were little, I would sing "A, You're Adorable," a song from my own childhood that was popular in the late 1940s. It starts with A ("you're adorable") and goes on to Z describing how wonderful the person is. It was a way for my children to learn the alphabet and a way for me to tell them how much they meant to me. You don't need to use the alphabet to inspire you to sing a love song to the special child in your life. Take any song with a name and insert your child's name instead, changing the words to fit her personality. My daughters liked hearing "their" songs, and I had fun making them up.

GOAL

Teaching by example that it is possible to make up your own songs

DIRECTIONS

Pick a song you like that has an easy tune. My song mind may be stuck in the 1940s, so I come up with "Rose Marie" and "Daisy, Daisy," but any song will do. Then just insert your own words. Don't worry if your words don't rhyme. Believe me, little ones don't care about that, they just love that you are singing about them! For example, if the tune is "Daisy, Daisy," and the child's name is Julien:

> Julien, Julien, here are my words so true
>
> I'm so happy to be so close to you
>
> I love the way you smile
>
> You're smart as you can be
>
> And every day, in every way
>
> You mean so much to me

Game 2: I Love You Because

GOALS

Self-esteem

Feedback on one's self

Learning about the qualities others admire

DIRECTIONS

Say these words to the child of your heart: "Do you know why I love you? I love you because _____." Fill in the blank with anything about the child you especially appreciate. You can be general or specific, as in "You are kind," or "You hugged your classmate when you saw she was upset."

VARIATION

Let your child know he merits love just by being himself by saying, "I love you because you are _____ (child's name)."

~~~~~~~~~~~~~~~~~~~~~~~~~~~~~~~~

Game 3: Secretary to the Writer

Many children love to make up stories. They also delight in having stories read to them. So imagine the thrill when the story they hear is their own.

GOALS

Self-esteem
Organizing thoughts

MATERIALS

A pen and paper or a computer, and a stapler and staples

DIRECTIONS

Get out your pen or word processor and let your budding writer know that you are interested in writing his story. You could arrange to have a writing session ahead of time or suggest it after he tells you about something that happened in his life. Stories could also be something he totally makes up, something he wishes would happen, or anything else.

Write all the words down, even if they don't make logical sense to you. Children's stories, like dreams, often have impossible things happen. To help him along, you could also ask such questions as "And then what happens?" "How did he feel about that?" "Was anyone else there?" "Where else would you like to go?" or "What did the other person say then?" Add a cover and staple the pages together down one side so it opens like a book. Read the story together many times.

VARIATION

Draw illustrations to go with the story. Make it a secret flap book by pasting sticky notes on top of the illustrations.

Game 4: Guess How Old

GOALS

Noticing visual and physical cues about people
Social and environmental awareness

DIRECTIONS

Ask your child to guess the ages of people, animals, and objects in her life. Include the people in the neighborhood or people on television or even characters in books. How old are the Cat in the Hat, Big Bird, and Barney anyway? Does anybody really know? How old are the nearby trees?

VARIATION

Give clues that help tell a person's age or information, like that some butterflies only live for a day whereas trees can live for hundreds of years. If you have a tree stump nearby, show how to count the rings to learn the age of the tree.

Game 5: Making Faces

GOALS

Imitation
Imagination
Controlling motor movement
Creativity

SETUP

Sit facing each other.

DIRECTIONS

Start with this question: "Can you do this with your face?" Then, for example, wink one eye and then the other. See if the child can do what you do.
Take turns trying out different possibilities, such as

+ Wiggling your ears
+ Curling your tongue
+ Raising one eyebrow
+ Touching your tongue to your nose
+ Crossing your eyes
+ Bobbing your Adam's apple
+ Making a raspberry sound with your
  lips

VARIATION

Make faces associated with different emotions, such as sad, tragic, happy,
elated, frustrated, and furious. Make animal faces, such as a fish face. What
would a turtle face look like? Take turns making any grotesque or silly face
and imitating each other.

Game 6: Pony Boy

GOALS

Awareness of body and movement in space
Control of the muscles of the upper body
Increased sense of balance

SETUP

Sit down and place your child on your knees, facing you.

DIRECTIONS

Start gently bouncing your knees up and down while you sing or chant:

"Pony boy, pony boy, won't you be my pony boy?"

Then change the motions by swinging your knees from side to side while singing:

"Don't say no, here we go."

Then, holding the child's arms, slowly lean him backward so his head is hanging upside down while you sing:

"Ride away with me."

VARIATION

You can modify the amount of movement with your child depending on how vigorously he likes to be tossed about. Some children really adore being tossed to and fro, whereas others like more gentle motion. You can always start slowly and then increase the amount of energy depending on the child's desire for action.

Game 7: Having a Disney Day

GOALS

Empathy
Appreciation for all the things that make up one's world

DIRECTIONS

Walt Disney knew how to capture children's attention by making inanimate things talk. Spend part of a day pretending everything is alive. Start the morning off in a fun way by saying, for example, "Hello, Mr. Coffee Pot. Thank you for making my morning brew for me." Encourage your cutie to ask the cereal bowl if she would mind holding some cereal and milk.

VARIATION

Go outside and talk to bugs. What do ants do for fun? Thank a tree for its shade.

Game 8: Knocking Game

GOALS

Listening
Focusing
Paying close attention
Learning auditory categories, such as "things that are metal sound like this"

MATERIALS

Objects to tap on that make different sounds, and a spoon (optional)

DIRECTIONS

With a child, listen to and identify the different sounds that objects make when you knock on them. Ask the child to close her eyes or turn her back to you. Then see if she can guess the object you are knocking on with your fist (or a spoon).

VARIATION

Take turns identifying the objects.

Game 9: Playing with Pebbles

GOALS

Learning about shapes
Experimenting with design
Fine motor skills

MATERIALS

Pebbles you find outside or the glass kind that you can buy at craft
    shops and dollar stores

DIRECTIONS

Put the pebbles in a large pile and use them to make different things, such as

- One large square
- Two small circles
- Two intersecting circles
- A triangle
- Two intersecting triangles, forming a star
- A body with arms and legs
- A road for a truck

VARIATIONS

1. There are many possibilities for this game, and kids will come up with some we haven't thought of. Take a photo, if you want, of the final results. Its beauty may surprise you.

2. If one of the variations your child eventually chooses involves

throwing, provide a bucket or plastic-lined wastebasket to throw into. She can practice her aiming and throwing skills, and you get the pebbles put away at the same time.

Game 10: How Many Hand Lengths?

GOALS

Estimating
Educated guessing

MATERIALS

Objects to measure

DIRECTIONS

Look at an object and have one child or a group of children guess how many hand lengths long it is using one child's hand size for the standard. Then have the child measure the length by placing her hand on the object and counting how many hands fit (measuring from a fingertip to the heel of her hand). Approximate fractions of a hand length, like a half or a quarter of a hand.

VARIATION

Use a foot as a measuring tool instead: "How many foot lengths long is it from the living room to the kitchen?"

Game 11: Edible Play-Doh

GOALS

Finger strengthening
Fine motor skills

MATERIALS

2 cups peanut butter, 2 cups powdered milk, and 1 cup honey; *or*

2 cups oatmeal, 1 cup flour, and ½ cup water

DIRECTIONS

All too often children want to eat Play-Doh, it looks that good. Rather than spend your energy trying to prevent this, make up a Play-Doh that you won't mind them eating, made from peanut butter or oatmeal.

Fun things for beginners to make with their Play-Doh are snakes (in which a slit is made in one end for a mouth), snowmen, and animals.

VARIATION

Try using "finger paint" that is safe to eat, such as ketchup, mayonnaise, prepared mustard, thickened gravy, and so on.

Count for Cooperation

You might not believe that such a simple approach as this one could be so effective, but I promise it works well. I have tried it with two-year-olds, four-year-olds, eight-year-olds, and twelve-year-olds with equal success.

It goes like this: "Let's see if you can run upstairs, get your shoes, and be back downstairs before I get to the number seven. Ready, go! One . . . two . . . three, four . . . five . . . six . . . good! You made it by six!"

Please note that this approach is quite the opposite from the old "I'll give you to ten to get those shoes, or you know what!" This is a game of challenge and speed that you could sometimes use for fun purposes. For example, "Let's see how long it takes you to run around the tree and touch the rock and come back. Ready, go!"

I have also used a timer: "Let's see if you can get your toys put away before the bell rings!" Although if the job is overwhelming, I might have to say instead, "Let's see how fast WE can . . ." and enter into the spirit of it.

I've had the tables turned on me. Once, my youngest said, "Can you run downstairs and bring me a glass of water before I count to ten and a half? One . . . two . . ." I took off.

It was fun to meet the challenge, and I noticed that it raised my energy level.

A stopwatch can be another fascinating touch. This technique has the added advantage for the older kids of actually teaching mathematical concepts, such as which number is bigger: "Look, you got the floor swept great, and you did it in two minutes and 49.6 seconds. That's 12 seconds less than yesterday, and you still did a good job. Oh, I'm lucky to have a helper as good as you!"

You might find, as I did, that children use this game idea on you to calm you down rather than speed you up. One day I was driving home from a long trip. It was rainy and dark, and the road was long and winding. The children had been cranky and fussy for a long while, and I wasn't feeling much better myself. I finally blew up at them to "Be quiet!"

The oldest child, then five years old, said serenely to me, "Do you think you could calm down by the time I count to seven? She began counting, "One . . . two . . ." When I realized what she was doing and my lips curled up in amusement, she said, "Good job! You did it by six!"

Games for Older Kids (Ages Seven to Fourteen)

Game 1: How Would You Describe Me?

GOALS

Feedback for self-awareness
Seeing others from a different perspective

MATERIALS

A pencil and paper

SETUP

Copy the following list of human characteristics, or write your own, and make a few copies: kind, patient, understanding, open minded, cheerful, optimistic, cute, lovely, loving, warm, loyal, thoughtful, generous, honest, wise, gentle, fair, funny, handsome, polite, respectful, sweet, silly, compassionate, sympathetic, intelligent, hard worker, peaceful, assertive, cooperative, beautiful, good athlete, dancer, artist, musician, careful, intelligent, charming, forceful, sensitive, good company, helpful, witty, good sense of humor.

DIRECTIONS

You and your partner have to circle the characteristic that best describes someone you both know. Do this with a number of people, and see if you pick the same characteristics. Talk about the choices made and why.

VARIATION

You each make a list about each other from the choices of characteristics and see how your choices match up by telling each other which characteristics were chosen. "You think I'm optimistic—why?" "You think I'm compassionate—awwwwww."

Game 2: Five Good Moments

GOALS

Developing a growing awareness of feeling
Knowing the kinds of things one enjoys

DIRECTIONS

Pick a day when you and your child will be apart for some of the day. Suggest that throughout the day you both look for five moments that make you feel good. The moment can be an interaction with someone, or something lovely that you saw or heard. What it is doesn't matter. What matters is that for at least a moment it made you feel good. Discuss all of your moments with your child.

VARIATIONS

1. Do it in the moment. Both look around and see or think of something that makes you feel good at that moment, no matter how mundane and ordinary or far-fetched and fantastical.

2. You can do this game with all the members of your family at the end of the day. Remind everyone in the morning. You could place a sticker on each person's hand as a reminder of the day's plan.

Game 3: Self-Portraits

GOALS

Noticing visual details
Fine motor skills

MATERIALS

A mirror, a felt marker, and a chair (optional)

SETUP

Sit or stand in front of a mirror.

DIRECTIONS

Have your child look in the mirror and, using a felt marker, draw exactly what she sees.

VARIATION

Sit across from one another and draw each other's faces on paper.

Game 4: People Report

GOAL

Noticing visual details and social cues

SETUP

Play this game at a store.

DIRECTIONS

Ask your child to look around at other people who are waiting in line near you at the store and silently notice as many details as he can. Tell him you will do the same. What are they wearing? What do you think their attitude is—are they patiently waiting, fidgety, distracted? Why do you think that? Report to each other once you are out of the store. It's fun to see how we focus in on different details coming from our own unique perspective.

VARIATIONS

1. If there are two people together, guess what their relationship is to each other and maybe even how they are getting along with each other.

2. Pretend there is someone in the line who is a spy, and you each have to figure out who it is. Later, outside the store, see if you both picked the same person.

Game 5: Which Line Is Best?

GOAL

Social awareness

SETUP

Play this game when you are in a line or about to get into a line.

DIRECTIONS

When picking a line at the grocery store, ease the frustration by betting on who picked the fastest line. You can be in the same line with your child, but keep an eye on where you would have been in another line and see which line reaches the checkout first. Notice details. Would the line with the older person or the woman with children be faster or slower?

VARIATION

Bet on the slowest line!

Game 6: Shadow Games

GOALS

Eye-foot coordination
Speed
Timing

SETUP

Play this game outside at dusk when you can see your shadows. This game can be played with two or more people.

DIRECTIONS

Have good fun romping by trying to step on each other's shadows.

VARIATION

Choose a specific part of the shadow to step on, such as the head or leg.

Game 7: Toe Stepping

GOALS

Concentration
Focusing
Practicing kindness
Empathy
Coordination

SETUP

Two people, either barefoot or wearing stockings, hold hands facing each other.

DIRECTIONS

Players try to step on the other's toes while at the same time keeping their toes from being stepped on. Remind players to step lightly. Golden rule: "Step on others as you would want to be stepped on."

VARIATION

Try it with three people!

Game 8: Stone Painting

GOALS

Experimenting with different designs
Creativity
Focusing

MATERIALS

Small rocks, paintbrushes, and water

DIRECTIONS

Painting lines on rocks with water can make anything look like elegant Japanese calligraphy. Use several rocks and experiment with different designs. No one has to worry about making a mistake because when it dries, it disappears!

VARIATION

If you don't want them to disappear, paint over the watermarks with paint.

Traveling Games

Game 1: Postcard Diaries

GOAL

Recording memories

MATERIALS

Postcards from different destinations, and pens, pencils, or crayons (or any other writing implements)

DIRECTIONS

When you take a trip with your child or even go somewhere in your own town, let your child select a postcard for that day or at each destination. She can write on the back of the postcard what she did on that day, and collect the postcards.

VARIATION

She can mail the postcards to herself and get a nice reminder, and then make a hole in one corner of each postcard and string them together.

Game 2: Travel Collections

GOALS

Noticing details
Memory recall
Writing

MATERIALS

A bag to hold memorabilia and a scrapbook

DIRECTIONS

Have your child collect small memorabilia during a trip, such as the wrapper from some exotic candy or the tickets to an interesting show. These can be pasted in a scrapbook when you get back home.

VARIATION

Have the child write a note about the meaning of each item of memorabilia and why it mattered or stood out to her.

The Honorable Head Garbage Taker-Outer

Here's a way to get a job done while making everyone feel important, necessary, and appreciated. I discovered it one day when I was hoping that my kids and their visitors might help me with a garden project of planting peas. I thought for sure they'd enjoy it, and was surprised when they seemed reluctant to join me in poking holes in the earth, dropping in the little round pea seeds, covering them, and pressing down the soil over them.

Then I remembered when it seemed like suddenly everyone in the workplace got new titles. The custodian became the maintenance engineer, and secretaries were assistant managers, and so on. . . . Same work, different titles. Yet the new titles were more respectful of the labor done. Janitors *do* maintain, and secretaries *do* manage.

I announced the positions available: "Let's see . . . for this work, I need an Honorable Hole Putter-Inner, a Gracious Seed Depositor, a Superior Soil Cover-Upper, and a Princely Press-It-Downer." I was delighted—and astonished—when everyone claimed a title and burst into activity.

Now, instead of asking someone, "Would you grate the potatoes?" I say, "You can be the Great Grater."

At a Head Start classroom I know, the teacher must also know this trick, because he gives out similar titles. The person who heads the line leading everyone to recess is the "Line Header." But the person who is even more important, the one who gets to say "Line up!" and watch the kids scurrying to follow his order by lining up in front of him, has a title too. He's the "Line Ender"!

CHAPTER TWO

~·~·~·~·

Games for Babies

Parenting is not about techniques and doing the "right" thing. It's about relationships. We all desire to have great connections with our children and to play with them; but if we weren't ourselves played with as children, it's not so easy to know what to do. One awareness that is so helpful is understanding that mental, motor, and social development is sequential, with one step building on another. All children progress, more or less, through the same stages, but each one grows at a different pace and in a different style. If you are the parent of more than one child, you don't need a scientist to tell you that no two babies are alike. One child may love movement and zooming around the room, whereas another may find exploring the tiniest things on the carpet so interesting. Same parents, different children. That is why this section has a variety of games to play with your child that are tailored to different personalities and interests, yet that all progress through the developmental stages by encouraging movement, exploration, and awareness.

Intelligence and coordination can be developed in a child from birth, and infants are eager to learn. They want to move so they can explore. Like little scientists, they want to investigate everything they come in contact with. The sensory system wants to know how an object looks, tastes, smells, feels, moves, and sounds. The brain wonders what happens if the object is dropped, shaken, or eaten, and what Mom's (or Dad's, or another caregiver's) response will be.

All this gathered information gives a baby's brain raw material to categorize, and it is the process of categorizing that develops the brain's ability to handle increasingly complex thought. The child who is allowed free rein to explore the environment, assuming, of course, that everything unsafe is out of reach, will have access to more material for the brain to process and thus will develop a greater ability to sort, process, and understand. Helping your baby develop these skills and abilities early in his life will make a strong and secure foundation on which to build advanced skills.

Muscles are also developed through use. The baby who has the whole floor to explore is going to have more practice crawling than the baby in a playpen. If there are stairs to go up or a box to climb in or a pillow to climb over, that baby is going to learn even more about coordinating muscle movements.

The point behind giving your baby these opportunities for movement and sensory exploration is not to hurry development but to deepen it and to enrich your attachment. When introducing an activity, be sure to have fun with it. If your baby is not interested, put it away, try again later, or forget it altogether. The important thing is that you enjoy one another. When being together and doing interesting things together is pleasurable—even if it's only a moment here and a moment there—both you and your child feel good about yourselves, and what is nicer than that?

What's in Grandma's Purse?

An Inquiring Toddler Wants to Know

If there is a grandma reading this—let's be real. There is NOTHING more interesting to a toddler than what is in your purse. Not even you. Do you remember the time when people in the press were questioning what was in the Queen of England's bag? We all wonder what people carry in their purse. Curious toddlers have none of that politeness that keeps us from looking. They will get right into your bag if they can. What is it that Grandma carries around? You can fight it and hide it away and make looking through your purse a clear "no-no." Or, you can purposely satisfy the child's curiosity by letting your bag be explored and even putting in some enticing items.

To protect your valued items, you could have a zippered bag of things you don't want the child to mess with, such as coins, bills, medicine, and so on. This you remove first and place out of reach.

What would a toddler find interesting? Such items as little bags of healthy treats, scarves, handkerchiefs, ribbons, spare keys, stickers, out-of-date credit cards, out-of-focus photos

you don't mind getting bent and mangled, an empty checkbook cover with slips of paper in the plastic pockets, little zippered purses, small books, a small note-book and pen, cotton balls, a toy magnifying glass—you get the idea. I figure if it won't hurt, it's a toy.

Of course, we grandmas can then take credit for all the natural learning that takes place with exploration. But the honest truth is simpler. While the toddler is exploring the purse, it's the per-fect moment to have an uninterrupted adult conversation with *your* child.

Game 1: Diaper Song

GOALS

Body awareness
Listening
Connecting

DIRECTIONS

When you are doing the morning routine of changing diapers and washing, sing about what you are doing (to the tune of "Alouette"):

> I'm wiping your tushie
> Your cute little tushie
> I'm wiping your bottom
> To make it all clean

VARIATION

Do this at bath time and sing about each body part.

Game 2: Helpful Legs

GOALS

Body awareness
Muscle memory
Receptive understanding of words

DIRECTIONS

Let baby help during diaper changing by doing a leg game that will teach her the actions that go with words.

Lift baby's legs up while saying:

"Legs go up up up up."

Then down while saying:

"Legs go dooooooown."

Repeat, repeat, repeat, and notice that baby will start to do it more and more on her own just by hearing you say the words:

"Legs go up up up up. Legs go dooooooown."

Do the same while opening and closing her legs to get her in position for changing:

"Legs go ooooooopen."

"And close!"

Repeat, repeat, repeat.

VARIATION

Passively put your child's arms and legs through the whole range of movement and sing along:

Your arms go up
Your arms go down
Your arms go in
And your arms go out

Do the same thing with ankles and wrists that go round and round.

Game 3: Pan Music

GOALS

Hearing stimulation
Eye-hand coordination
Practicing with rhythm

MATERIALS

Objects in kitchen cupboards, such as a pan, plastic bowl, spoon, and
oatmeal container

DIRECTIONS

Take out a metal pan or things like an oatmeal container and an upside-
down plastic bowl. Make a little rhythm as you hit them. Or put your child
in front of you and put a spoon in his hand, with your hand over his, as you
make a little rhythm together.

VARIATIONS

1. Point out the differences between the sounds that are made when you
   hit the metal pan and the sounds made when you hit the plastic bowl.
2. Try out different rhythms. Show baby how "ba ba boom" sounds different from "boom ba ba ba."

Game 4: Homemade Rattles

GOALS

Hearing stimulation
Visual stimulation

MATERIALS

Small, empty containers with lids, and different materials for filling them

DIRECTIONS

Make interesting rattles by filling empty and cleaned pill containers or travel shampoo bottles with different materials, such as pennies, salt, sand, beans, or rice. Tighten each closed lid. These various bottles will each make a different sound when shaken, and they are just the right size for baby's hand.

VARIATION

Add color to items like rice, sand, and salt using food coloring or paint.

Game 5: Clap a Rhythm

GOALS

Hearing rhythm
Coordinating movement
Connecting

DIRECTIONS

Because speech is made up of rhythm, a good way to practice a pre-speech skill is to try out different ways to clap your hands with your baby. Experiment with different rhythms.

VARIATION

Experiment with different ways you and baby can clap your hands together, such as high five, low five, and slide five.

Game 6: Bird Talk

GOALS

Hearing stimulation
Distinguishing between different frequencies

DIRECTIONS

Sit outside, especially in the early morning and at dusk when the birds sing the most, and listen together. Try to find the bird that is singing.

VARIATION

Try to imitate the sounds you hear. Doves have a long call, whereas other birds chirp.

Game 7: Hand Dancing

GOALS

Hearing variations
Feeling rhythm

DIRECTIONS

Put on some music, take your baby's hands, and move to the rhythm of the sounds. Some types of music invoke a swaying movement, and others make you want to move your hands faster.

VARIATION

Pick your baby up and dance to the rhythm.

The Talking Hand

Children have selective hearing. They might be able to hear a piece of candy being unwrapped in the next room but miss your mentioning that it was time to clean up. Sometimes the way to get them to pay attention is to introduce novelty. Novelty in this case is that instead of you talking, it's Mr. Hand.

Using your four flexed fingers as the top of the mouth and your thumb as the bottom, introduce your child to Mr. Hand.

Your introduction, for example, may sound like this:

"Hey, Jacob, I want you to meet someone. Mr. Hand, say hi to Jacob."

"Hi, Jacob." (You say hi while working your thumb up and down as if it is the bottom lip. Your fingers stay still and bent. You can even draw a pair of eyes on the side of your index finger to make Mr. Hand more authentic.) "Hey, Jacob, wanna flick a penny back and forth?" (Or you could say, "Want to pat my head?" or "Wanna thumb wrestle?" or "Can I play what you're playing?" or any other activity or conversation that engages the child with Mr. Hand.) Remember to look at your hand as if you were looking at another being, too.

If Mr. Hand has an interesting accent, that adds to the fun and makes him more of a separate character from you!

Bring Mr. Hand out whenever you are wanting more attention and cooperation. I find that sometimes kids will do things for Mr. Hand that they wouldn't do for me, like clean up together.

Once the child knows Mr. Hand, bring him out when you need your child to focus on something. For example, you've already asked him twice if he was ready to eat, and he was too absorbed in something else to answer. Bring out Mr. Hand and have him ask the question.

The children on the autism spectrum who tend to avoid eye contact might sometimes be more comfortable talking with Mr. Hand.

Mr. Hand could also provide the element of the unexpected that would capture the attention of the child whose attention is scattered.

Mainly, Mr. Hand is your friend because he can lighten up a moment and still help you get the cooperation you need!

Game 8: Silly Sounds

GOALS

Awareness of sounds
Hearing differences between sounds
Imitation

DIRECTIONS

Make different sounds with your voice for your baby to imitate—try high, squeaky sounds like "eee eee eee," or low, throaty sounds like "oooooo." Speak loudly, talk quietly, whisper, and hum.

VARIATION

Make up silly gestures to go with the sounds. Encourage imitation. For some children it's helpful to put your hands on their hands and make the movements together.

Game 9: Swat at This

GOALS

Increased shoulder, arm, and hand muscle control
Enhanced eye-hand coordination

MATERIALS

Objects to hang: for instance, bells; a stuffed small bag made with crinkly paper, such as a potato chip bag; plastic bracelets; corks; a stuffed sock with a face drawn on it; measuring spoons; tinfoil balls; shells too big to swallow; a squeaky toy; a small stuffed animal; clothespins; plastic net bath scrubbers; napkin rings; canning rings; plastic or wooden spoons; empty toilet paper rolls; feathers; plastic eggs (with noisemakers inside, taped or glued shut); yarn pom-poms; fabric strips cut with pinking shears; and sponges

SETUP

Where to hang the toys depends on where baby spends a lot of time. You can hang toys from the top handle of an infant seat or swing. You can put a hook in the ceiling above the diaper changing table and hang toys from that.

You can use a commercial toy gym that has toys hanging from it and replace them with a changing variety of new toys.

You want the toys to hang enticingly but securely in front of the child so that she will reach out to swat or grab them.

DIRECTIONS

Hang objects for baby to swat at and eventually grab. The variety is endless. What you hang doesn't matter as long as it is safe. Baby is interested in everything. Change the objects once or twice a month to keep the game fresh. Add bells and other noisemakers to add sounds to the visual stimulation. Noisemakers have the added advantage of allowing you to hear what is being played with even when you are not watching.

Game 10: Feelings, Nothing More Than Feelings

GOALS

Tactile stimulation
Visual stimulation

MATERIALS

Different kinds of materials that can be either squished or swirled, such as yogurt or cornstarch

SETUP

Place baby in a high chair with a tray or in his chair at the table.

DIRECTIONS

Put materials that feel different on the tray or table to swish around, such as cornstarch, baby powder, whipped cream, yogurt, or shaving cream. (Use only edible materials if your child still puts everything in her mouth.)

VARIATION

Add color to the materials using ketchup for red, mustard for yellow, and soy sauce for brown. Or use these materials by themselves for finger painting fun.

Game 11: Catch a Moving Cube

GOALS

Eye-hand coordination
Receiving new tactile information
Focusing

MATERIALS

Ice cubes

SETUP

Place baby in a high chair with a tray.

DIRECTIONS

Put an ice cube on the tray. Baby will be fascinated as she tries to catch the moving cube. When the cube gets small, replace it with a fresh big cube so it will always be too big to swallow.

VARIATION

Float Ping-Pong balls in baby's bath or put dabs of shaving cream in the bath water.

Game 12: Move Me Around

GOALS

Expanding visual perception

Increasing vocabulary

DIRECTIONS

Place baby in various safe areas in the house: on the living room floor, in an infant seat on the kitchen table, or in a cozy corner of the couch.

VARIATION

Take baby for a tour of the house and yard by pointing out one thing and another.

Game 13: In Your Face

GOALS

Control of eye muscles

Control of tongue muscles

Eye scanning

Listening

DIRECTIONS

Because the most interesting thing to a baby is a human face, stick your face up close to hers and then slowly move it in various directions: side to side, back and forth, near and far.

VARIATION

Hum sounds to go with the movements.

Making Faces with Lance

I didn't like Lance. As a therapist, I don't like to admit this, but, at first, I thought Lance was exceedingly, excruciatingly dull. He seemed to be not in his own interesting world, but just oblivious to ours. His mother, however, thought he was the cat's pajamas. If you weren't born in the 1940s that compliment makes no sense, but trust me, she thought the moon rose and set on her baby. Even though she had a house full of children and Lance was three years old, he was to her, her darling baby boy. She did everything for him, and he entered the Head Start program without the ability to even wash his hands by himself.

We had to start at step one and teach him how to follow basic requests that are useful at school, such as "Come here," "Sit down," "Stand up," and "Walk this way." His aide, Marlon, and I started his lessons by having him come to us when asked. Marlon and I stood five feet apart and took turns calling his name and gesturing for him to come to us. When he did, needing a prompting nudge from one person and the clue of seeing arms held out by the other, Lance was rewarded with a hug. He liked that and started to get the idea, and he began to go toward the beckoning person with a certain measure of glee that began to warm up my heart a little toward him.

Because imitation is crucial to learning, we then tried to get him to imitate our movements. We showed him how to clap his hands, slap his thigh, and wiggle his fingers, but he seemed not to have a clue how to do these things or how to copy us. Then I tried the one skill that I always do with infants. It's the skill that fascinates little babies, and the one that they will, even at as young as three months, try to copy. I stuck my tongue out. Lance surprised me by sticking his tongue out. Yeah! I blew my lips and made a raspberry sound. Lance did too! I wagged my tongue back and forth. So did Lance. Lance, it turned out, had his own sounds that he could make, and we copied him. And then Lance gave us the first biggest grin I ever saw him do, and at that moment I saw what his mother saw. Lance was adorable.

Later, Lance was part of the group that learned a new song with movements. The purpose of the song was to teach children about syllables and that every syllable has a beat. We start off with a game in which each child says his or her name, and then we all clap out the beats. Brad has one beat, for example, and Jennifer has three. Then we get up and walk around the room moving our bodies to the beat of the words. I didn't expect Lance to get the concept of syllables, but I was delighted to see that he thoroughly enjoyed doing the movement game. It's sung to the tune of "Frère Jacques," and goes like this:

Watermelon (stomping feet while taking four steps forward—one step for each syllable)

Watermelon (four more)

Cantaloupe (three jumps forward)

Cantaloupe (three more)

Apples and banana (six steps done in place very quickly)

Apples and banana (again six more)

Grapes (turn in a circle)

And pears (jump in place)

Grapes (turn in a circle again)

And pears (jump in place again)

Lance may have needed some assistance in knowing when to turn in a circle, but he didn't need help knowing how to enjoy it all. He laughed and giggled right along with the others in the delight of everyone moving and jumping together and in the end, finally and fully, won my heart.

Game 14: Keep Your Eyes on This

GOALS

Encouraging the control of the six muscles that move each eye
Coordinating the movement of both eyes together
Distinguishing between what is figure and what is background

MATERIALS

A variety of objects, such as helium balloons and ribbons

SETUP

Place objects around the room for baby to look at. They could hang from a hook in the ceiling or be objects that can be seen out the window.

DIRECTIONS

Hang interesting things above the bed or changing table that move, such as crepe paper, feathers, scarves, a balloon, and ribbons. Release helium balloons up to the ceiling and let the strings dangle. Change objects from time to time to retain the novelty. Other ideas are to place a bird feeder outside of a nearby window so baby can watch the avian action, or hang a hummingbird feeder full of red sugar water. Place a fish tank in view so that baby can watch the fish swim.

VARIATION

Try other things that might make interesting sounds knocking together, or that might just be interesting to look at, such as decorated Ping-Pong balls, spools of thread, flowers, cigar tubes, plastic fruit, aluminum pie plates, and a stuffed glove.

Game 15: Tender Touches

GOALS

Tactile stimulation

Awareness of others

DIRECTIONS

Rub, stroke, massage, squeeze, and pat baby's body to send stimulating information to the brain.

VARIATIONS

1. Rub baby's body with different textures: silk, velvet, feathers, wool, and cotton balls.

2. Make a quilt of different textures for baby to lie on.

3. Kiss the soles of baby's feet. Babies delight in being kissed all over!

Game 16: Smell Sorting

GOALS

Identification of smells

Awareness of objects in the environment

MATERIALS

Different items that have interesting smells, such as herbs, flowers, spices, lotions, coffee, vanilla, and coconut oil

DIRECTIONS

Put different items near baby's nose for smelling. While cooking, waft spices by her nose and talk about what they are. Have her smell fragrances you are using in the bathroom.

Take walks at different times of the day to experience the feel and smell of morning frost, afternoon sun, and spring and autumn days.

Game 17: Describe That Taste

GOALS

Taste bud discrimination
Experiencing sharing food

MATERIALS

Small amounts of different foods, such as salt crackers, pickles, honey, and sauces

SETUP

Sit beside your child and share food.

DIRECTIONS

Make a plate of different types of food and give small pieces to your child for him to try. Have a bite too. Describe the tastes as baby tries them: sweet, salty, hot, cold, sour.

VARIATION

Describe the textures of the foods: crunchy, sticky, smooth, chewy, silky, wet, dry.

Game 18: Speaking in Sounds

GOALS

Monitoring one's own sounds

Imitation

DIRECTIONS

Repeat back sounds to baby that he makes. Go back and forth making sounds. Let baby know you are listening to him and that you speak his language.

Make nonsense sounds for baby to imitate: raspberries, tongue clucking, humming.

Game 19: Sound Sorting

GOALS

Hearing stimulation

Sound identification

DIRECTIONS

Take baby on a tour of the house, knocking on different objects to hear the different sounds they make.

VARIATION

Point out the sounds in the house and neighborhood: a toilet flushing, a truck rumbling by, and a doorbell ringing.

Game 20: Box Ride

GOALS

Balance awareness

Developing joint attention

MATERIALS

A cardboard box

DIRECTIONS

Put baby in a box on the floor. Push her around like the box is a car, or rock the box like it is a boat.

VARIATION

Make sounds like a moving car or a rocking boat, or sing appropriate songs like "Row, Row, Row Your Boat."

Game 21: Pillow Pile

GOALS

Planning motor movements

Muscle strength

Achieving a goal

MATERIALS

Pillows

SETUP

Pile pillows below a window.

DIRECTIONS

Let baby crawl up on the pillows and look outside. (Make sure baby can't get out of the window.)

VARIATION

Place pillows and books on the floor in the baby's path, for her to crawl up and over.

- - - ˅ - ˅ - ˅ - ˅ - ˅ - ˅ - ˅ - ˅ - ˅ - ˅ - ˅ -

Game 22: Beach Ball Bounce

GOALS

Trunk strength
Sitting balance

MATERIALS

A beach ball

DIRECTIONS

Sit baby on top of a beach ball. Holding him by his hips, slowly move him from side to side and back and forth, and gently bounce him up and down.

VARIATION

With baby sitting on your lap, hold him by his hips and use your legs to move him from side to side and up and down.

Chalk and the Bubbie

My grandson dumped the whole box of chalk onto the pavement. It was one of those BIG boxes, and the chalk was already broken into many pieces from previous use.

I sighed inside. I knew he knew that his mother didn't let him get out of cleaning up his own messes, but would his Bubbie, his grandma?

It didn't look as if he meant to make a mess at first. He was searching inside the box for the size of chalk he wanted and the pieces began to fall out. And then, it seemed like the combination of the thrill of doing something sorta wrong and the beauty of seeing them all fall like snow, with just a little nudge, was irresistible.

I did not want to get irritated. We had just had this, to me, stupendous moment. We had been in the house, and he was playing on a fake guitar, making sounds and strumming. His one-year-old brother came toddling over and contributed his rhythmic ability by banging his hand on top of the strings. His brother, two years his senior, hit him.

The Bubbie stepped in, and I felt I had gotten it all right, empathizing with the three-year-old who had his play disrupted, appreciating the younger boy's need to participate. Cleverly I got a turn-taking game started by going first on the guitar and making up a silly tune; then we all got silly and had fun watching what the other one would come up with on his turn.

I was feeling like super-Grandma, which is always a setup for being brought down.

Any psychologist would have applauded me for the superb way I turned the guitar moment from bad to good with my grandsons. But, as is so often the case, instead of applause, I got the next challenge: Could I make my grandson pick up all the chalk and still keep things pleasant? Where was my energy reserve to come up with something?

"You're going to have to put all those back, Oliver," I said.

"No, I don't," he said, and got up and walked into the house, over and past the scattered chalk pieces.

I felt tired. I felt humbled. I wasn't that good at this after all.

I sat there on the concrete porch stairs. A piece of chalk was still in my hand from the original game I thought we went outside to play—drawing on the front sidewalk.

I sat there and scribbled just to have a quiet moment before I'd have to get up and get Oliver to go back to his duty.

But my daughter had trained him well, and Oliver came back outside. Without a word, he went down the stairs to where the empty box lay and began to put the pieces in. Not silently; he rarely does anything silently, especially if he's playing with cars. Instead he started counting in rhythm: "One, two, three, one, two three, one, two, three," he'd count off, putting a piece of chalk away on each one count. I watched him, fascinated and relieved, and then it came to me to join the band. One, two, three, one, two, three—my feet stomped out the rhythm; my hands clapped it too. We slowed it down, we sped it up: one . . . two . . . three . . . one . . . two . . . three . . . one-two-three, one-two-three.

The work got done. The box was filled. We were smiling.

Oliver may never remember this experience, and there were still plenty of challenging times ahead, but for me it is a precious memory of a capital *M* Moment I had with my grandson.

Game 23: Standing and Counting

GOALS

Balance
Shifting weight
Recovering balance

DIRECTIONS

When baby feels close to being able to stand independently, make a game out of seeing how long she can stand. Keeping your hands ready to catch her, stand her up and count out loud with excitement for each second she can stand alone. "One, two, three, four, five! Wow!"

VARIATION

Make a game of gently pushing baby from side to side while standing, helping her learn how to shift weight from one leg to the other (a prewalking skill).

Game 24: Furniture Pathway

GOALS

Balance
Leg strength

SETUP

Set up the furniture so that baby can walk, for example, from the couch to the coffee table, to a side chair, and then to your chair (and arms).

DIRECTIONS

A baby who's started walking and can only do two or three steps alone can feel a sense of independence if he can walk a short distance on his own. Pieces of furniture placed near each other can make a trail he can negotiate.

VARIATION

Encourage baby to walk from one end of the couch to the other by putting something enticing on the end.

Game 25: Backward Steps

GOALS

Balance

Leg strength

DIRECTIONS

Let baby hold on to your clothes as you walk backward in tiny steps.

VARIATION

Walk sideways with baby holding on to you.

Game 26: Book in a Baggie

GOALS

Social awareness

Learning names of people in one's life

Increasing vocabulary of descriptive words

Answering "who" and "what" questions

MATERIALS

Photos, sandwich bags, a pen, and either a stapler and staples or ties

SETUP

Put photos of family members in individual plastic sandwich bags and staple or tie them together as if they are pages in a book. Title the front page of the book *People Who Love You*.

DIRECTIONS

"Read" the book to baby by naming the people in the photos and describing what is happening, such as "This is Grandma laughing," or "This is your brother Max playing with a ball."

VARIATION

Put a sticky note over the photo so that the child can guess whose photo is there before lifting the flap. Give her clues like "This is someone who lives next door" or "This is someone who loves to play ball with you."

Rings on a Stick (or Something Similar)

My fourteen-month-old grandson, Julien, was beginning to get bored with my fill-and-dump games. He had put marbles in a hole poked in the top of a yogurt container; he had put pennies in a piggy bank and poker chips in slots. He was ready for a game that required a bit more finesse. I got out the game that is next on the developmental checklist: stacking rings. You know the one, with the pole and a variety of things—wooden discs, cloth rings, foam doughnuts—to put on it. Julien didn't put them on in order of size, but he got the idea and put them all on. I wanted to expand his experiences in putting other types of rings on poles.

I decided to do a homemade version of that game with materials I had on hand, which were,

perhaps oddly enough, popsicle sticks and those little gold-colored rings that hold the papers in a binder together. The kind you'd get at an office supply store. I had a bunch of them.

It was a beautiful summer day, and I stuck the popsicle sticks in a small flower pot, filled with dirt. I showed him how to put the rings on the stick.

Julien was not getting this game, however. He didn't seem to notice my great demonstration of putting golden rings on the popsicle sticks. Instead, he decided that taking the popsicle sticks out of the flower pot and fitting them through the space between the boards on the deck was a better game. He watched as they disappeared between the slots and onto the dirt below. I smiled weakly as he dismantled my original game with an original game of his own.

Once the popsicle sticks had been dispatched into the cracks he, at last, noticed the rings. He picked one up and looked at it from different angles. He was squatting, and he also looked down at his undiapered, free-as-the-wind bottom. It was summer, and he was learning about toileting. He noticed that he had a stick-like protuberance of his own. He eyed the ring, eyed his penis, and put the ring on it. He did it perfectly.

See, I knew he was of the age to learn that skill, I just didn't have the right equipment. He did.

Game 27: Straws in a Bottle

GOALS

Finger dexterity

Eye-hand coordination

Focused attention

MATERIALS

A water bottle, drinking straws, and scissors

SETUP

Cut straws into small pieces. One straw will make about four pieces.

DIRECTIONS

Use an empty plastic water bottle with the cap removed and show baby how to put straw pieces in the opening. Once all the straw pieces are used, shake the bottle and pour them out—or let the child do that—and repeat the game.

VARIATIONS

1. Instead of straw pieces, use toothpicks. To make it more challenging, keep the cap on and poke a hole in the cap that is the diameter of a toothpick.

2. Instead of straw pieces, use dried, large beans, such as lima beans, as long as baby won't put beans in her nose or ears.

Game 28: Nest the Cans

GOALS

Awareness of size differences
Eye-hand coordination

MATERIALS

Empty, clean cans of different sizes (such as small tomato paste, medium peas, and large fruit cans) with the edges pressed down so they are not sharp

SETUP

Fit the cans inside each other from smallest to largest, having the child watch you do this.

DIRECTIONS

Have baby place the cans inside each other or stack them from the largest to the smallest. Start with the largest and the smallest, and then, when that is easy, introduce the middle sizes.

VARIATION

Nest measuring cups.

Game 29: Voice-Over

GOALS

Communication
Increasing vocabulary of descriptive words
Understanding sequences

DIRECTIONS

Describe what you are doing while you are doing it. "Mommy is pouring water in the coffee maker. Now I'm putting ground coffee in the filter. I'm flipping on the switch and making coffee. Listen . . . hear the coffee coming out? See it? Mommy made coffee."

VARIATION

Describe activities the child is doing while they are happening. Think of how the broadcasters on a nature program describe what the viewers are seeing. Describe the action of the cat or anything moving. Ask the child for input ("What is the spider doing?"), or instead of saying what someone or something is doing, sing it with made-up lyrics!

Game 30: Chip Bank

GOALS

Fine motor skills
Awareness of rotating wrist
Increasing attention span
Completing tasks
Eye-hand coordination

MATERIALS

A large plastic container and poker chips (or small cardboard squares cut to fit into the slot, or large coins that are too big to swallow), and a cutting implement

SETUP

Cut a slot in the lid of any large plastic container as if it were a "piggy bank."

DIRECTIONS

Show the child how to slip poker chips into the slot, one at a time. Lift the lid off when the container is full or there are no more chips, dump out the chips, replace the lid, and begin again. When the child is able, have her open the container and dump out the chips.

Game 31: Color Matches

GOALS

Learning differences between colors
Matching things that are the same

MATERIALS

Paint samples (two of each color) from the hardware store or paint shop, paper (optional), and glue (optional)

SETUP

Place one paint sample of each color on the table, or paste the samples onto a piece of paper.

DIRECTIONS

Place the paper with the samples on it in front of your child or just have your child look at the samples set on the table. Give your child matching samples, one at a time, and ask her to put each one on top of the color that is the same.

Start with two or three choices and add more later.

VARIATION

Make your own samples by coloring sticky notes with crayons. Have your child help make them, or ask an older sibling to make them for a younger sibling.

Small Is Nice Too

There is a form of praise we give our children that has always bothered me—and I use it all the time. It's when we praise our children for being big, as in "What a BIG girl you are."

Some children might glow from hearing those words, but I suspect their pleasure is more from our positive tone than from any innate pride about being BIG. For what does being bigger entail, really? All that is required is that one gets older, and getting older is hardly a personal accomplishment.

It's something like that "My how you have grown" comment, which is almost impossible to resist saying to a child you haven't seen for a while. I remember hating it as a child and thinking sarcastically to myself, "Well, what do you expect me to do—shrink?"

But as annoying as "My how you have grown" can be, it still doesn't have the underlying sting to it that "What a BIG boy you are" does. That one implies that being big is a wonderful thing to be. So, what does that say about being small? That it is a lousy thing to be, or at the very least not as good as being big?

I realize when I let that phrase come tumbling out of my mouth that I am, in fact, being verbally lazy. I could more accurately say, for example, "You've really learned how to brush you teeth well. I see you are even brushing the ones in the back now!" instead of the generic "What a BIG girl you are!" praise. That way, instead of congratulating her for growing, I have given her some recognition for improving a skill.

But it's hard to remember to do that. First I have to stop and think about what is so great about what she did, and, worse, I have to break the habit of automatically praising "big behavior." I'm not always successful, and I used to hope that my children didn't pick up on the "small is not good" hidden message. But one day, when my youngest was little, she let me know she heard the latent message loud and clear.

At the time she was being weaned to her own bed from the family bed, and I was trying to convince her to spend the whole night there and cease her nightly 2:00 a.m. journey into our bed. "Big girls sleep all night long in their beds. Your sister sleeps all night long in her bed. She's a big girl," I unnecessarily added.

"I big girl too," said my then two-and-a-half-year-old, her curls bouncing as she nodded her head vigorously in agreement. "I sleep all night in bed," she promised.

We kissed good night; she closed her large blue eyes and laid her chubby cheek on her pillow.

I had second thoughts. What if she really did stop making those nightly excursions to our bed? I would miss that cuddly little body snuggling against me, her comforting hand stroking my hair, her cupid lips softly smiling at me.

I went to bed that night thinking about how time passes and things inevitably change. At 2:00 a.m. that night, just like always, I heard those little feet padding toward me.

"I just a yiddle girl," she tearfully apologized.

"I am so glad," I whispered to her, enfolding her into my arms and kissing away the tears from her soft cheeks, "I am so glad."

Progressive Games for Ages Three to Seven

In this section there are progressive games for children ages three to seven that use one kind of material, such as plastic water bottles, to provide a variety of games. Progressive games keep changing to challenge different skills. There are two goals for the children. One goal is to enhance one or more of the domains—social, sensory, cognitive, or communication. The other goal is larger: to create community. Having community, feeling a sense of belonging, being included just the way we are, is a strong need for all humans. Our survival brains are wired to crave connection.

Processing the world differently or having physical challenges or different mental capacities, however, can sometimes make it hard for everyone to fit in.

Every game in this chapter encourages shared attention, in which everybody is paying attention to the same thing at the same time. The games give everyone the possibility of joining in and finding connection through play.

One Goal for Teachers, Therapists, Aides, and Caregivers

There is only one goal for the adults, the special education and mainstream teachers, aides, parents, community workers, and related service therapists. That goal is to be aware that a large variety of skills can be encouraged with only one simple material.

In my over forty years of experience, which includes playing with children all over the world, I discovered that it doesn't take much to engage children in healthy play and that all children like the same kinds of things. For example, when working with children at a school for the deaf in Laos, our main resource was newspapers. By rolling them up into "bats," we were able to jump over them, leap between them, throw them at targets, toss them in the air, incorporate them into a dance, and have other forms of creative fun that enhanced basic motor skills, sensory integration, and dynamite social interaction.

Another example: when working with children at a Head Start center, I needed to include two children on the autism spectrum, one child with the diagnosis of attention deficit/hyperactivity disorder (ADHD) and another child with visual impairments. I had a blanket. Small groups at a time got wrapped in that blanket and jumped together. Individually they each experienced being turned into a burrito as well as rocked in a sling. Everyone worked together to form a trampoline for a stuffed doll and count the number of bounces. The children on the spectrum loved the deep touch, the child with ADHD really appreciated all the movement, and the child with visual impairments enjoyed the tactile stimulation. They all laughed, squealed, and enjoyed the moments together.

Many games, only one material.

What Materials Are Best?

Materials that are easy to get, such as aluminum cans, string, and plastic water bottles, are convenient and gentle on the budget. They can be quite diverse in their uses and have the eco-friendly aspect of being reused recyclables.

But many other objects can be candidates for play. I found an inexpensive bamboo ladder at a home decorating store that was meant to hold towels. I thought, *Why not try this?* Turns out I came up with quite a few ideas for ways to jump and hop in the spaces between—and balance on—the rungs of the ladder, and I thought that I had probably come up with all possible variations. Then I asked the children if they had any ideas for additional games, and they surprised me by coming up with a whole slew of new ones.

Surely, I thought, *there can be no other possibilities*, but another teacher, not seeing the games we played, did what she thought we had done and came up with a brand new idea! See the Ladder Games if you want the details, but get the message: many things can make good game materials.

The Upside of Making Your Own Educational Toys

I remember the first time I bought an educational toy. It was a shape sorter in which the square block fits in the square hole, the ball in the round hole, and so on. I worried that the toy had only one square, one ball, and so forth, and if my children ran true to form, those parts would disappear within minutes.

Roxanne lost the square immediately, and the puppy chewed the ball. I wrote an irate letter to the toy manufacturer pointing out its error. I expected a letter of apology and a notice of the company's intentions to add spare parts to future toys. I got back, instead, a price list. For two dollar each (!) plus shipping, I could purchase more parts.

I've discovered since then that a lot of learning toys can be made in my own kitchen using nothing more complicated than scissors, colored paper, and glue. For instance, when I wanted to teach my children about colors, I would use colored paper and make two squares of each color (an index card was my template). I'd have two yellow, two blue, two green, and so on. At first, I'd lay out two cards and say, "Here are two cards. One is red, and the other is blue. Now here is another red card. Please put this red card on top of the other red card." I'd help guide their hand to the correct pile at first until they caught on. Later, I'd lay out all the colors and ask them to "put the card on the one that is the same color." As they got older and I wanted to introduce words like "puce" and "teal," I'd "borrow" matching paint samples from the hardware store for the game. Because puzzle pieces often went awry, I would sometimes make my own by using the sides of cereal boxes. I would cut the picture up in a number of pieces—more as they got older—and let them put it back together.

However, a homemade educational toy can be as simple as cutting out the basic shapes of circle, square, and triangle and having your learner place them on top of the matching drawn or cut-out shapes.

The great thing about these games is that they provided some quality time between my children and me. The children seemed to relish these moments. It's important to emphasize that these are games and NOT tests. I am happy to supply answers. The object is not just to help children learn, although that will be happening, or to increase their awareness, although that too will be happening, but mostly to do something enjoyable together, which is always nice when it happens.

How to Organize the Kids

Because many of the games involve turn taking, children can, of course, stand behind each other in the more traditional sense of lining up, but sometimes standing behind another can inspire pushing, wrestling, and cutting ahead of one's place in line.

There are other possibilities that make turn taking itself into a game:

- *The line faces the action.* Stand children in a line so everyone is looking at what is happening. Use the physical boundaries to help define the action wanted. For example, if there is a wall to define the space, say, "Place your back to the wall and face the rug." As each child has his or her turn, the line moves sideways.

When the children are turned sideways in a line facing the action, everyone's attention will be involved, and children just need to be reminded to move the line sideways.

- *Everyone sits in a circle.* This can work well with groups used to such activities as morning circle. Everyone has a front-row seat to watch the action in the middle.

- *Everyone sits in chairs.* Have a chair for each child. Sitting in a chair gives the children each a "home" of their own, so to speak. This works well if your group tends to be a bit on the rowdy side. Having a seat makes it easier for children to contain their excitement by reducing their choices of ways to move and interact. Explain at the start that every child will get more than one turn. It helps to make the rule that only children who are sitting will be chosen to be next (for example, "Jilly is sitting quietly, so she gets to go next"). Or establish the rule that children will take turns starting with one end of the line and going one by one to the other end. In this way they know that their turn is coming, which helps them develop patience!

How to Get and Maintain Attention

◆ *Establish listening skills right away.* Say, for example, "If you are listening to me, you have your baby finger on your cheekbone." Then look around to see who has followed the instruction and say, for instance, "Liam is listening. Claire is listening. They have their baby fingers on their cheekbones."

Continue giving a series of directions until all children show they are listening. This can be a great time to introduce new names of body parts, such as "pointer finger to ear lobe," or to reinforce lessons, such as knowing right from left ("Put your right elbow on your left knee").

◆ *Give clues.* A fun way to keep children acutely listening that I learned from speech pathologist Teresa Caraway is to choose the child whose turn is next by giving clues. "I'm choosing someone who is wearing plaid pants and a shirt that is the color of an apple." Everyone looks around to see who fits that description, which reinforces social awareness and, in this example, color association and new words ("plaid"). There is no end to descriptions you can use, such as "a person whose name has three syllables and starts with the sound 'Ja'" (Jennifer) or "the person who loves to play basketball."

Using this method, children never know if they will be the ones called and will be quite attentive to the descriptive words! They also will be very aware of each other as they try to figure out whose turn is next.

How to Organize the Games

Be clear about where the game starts and where it ends. A mat or piece of colored paper can mark where the children are to stand when they are throwing or where to begin the activity when they are being active.

It's also helpful to have a mat or piece of paper to show where the activity ends. This is especially useful because you often want to have the children go from point A to point B rather than leave it open ended about where they are to jump or move to.

How to Get Everyone Involved

Singing a song that pertains to the action helps the other players stay attentive when it is not their turn and keeps everyone involved.

Cheerleading is another way. Sometimes chanting a child's name in encouragement is what's best. For example, when Victor is jumping over the bottles, the class chants, "Victor! Victor! Victor! Victor!" and then applauds at his success.

How to End the Game

If children have been waiting their turn and have had two or three turns each, they can start to get antsy. It's time to end the waiting-for-your-turn phase and let everyone go at the same time. If you are jumping over cans, for example, spread them out into a large circle so that the children can keep jumping without waiting. The wider the circle, the less likely the kids are to have a traffic jam. Another fun ending is to let children make up their own activity with the material that was used. You can have them work in small groups to prepare a new idea for the others or just have them each spontaneously come up with something on their own, which they would introduce one at a time. Everyone would then get to try out the new idea.

The "Bring Me" Game

There are many others who like to add games to their time with kids. One is Montessori teacher Rita Bonnici, who uses a game when the kids in her class are outdoors to burn up some of their energy and give them something different to do. As in a "treasure hunt," children get to explore and find treasured items.

As a grandmother, I like this game because no matter how much energy we old-timers have, little ones still have more. This game levels the field because the adult gives instructions and the children run around. This gives us quiet moments to sit, relax, and soak up some sun while appreciating how clever the children are.

The first step is to present a challenge. It can be simple, as in "Can you bring me four leaves?" If more than one child, give separate instructions to each. How detailed your requests are can fit the child ("four small leaves" as opposed to "four leaves"). When the child returns with four leaves, or instead with a bunch of leaves, you count out four. Compliment his accomplishment with specific praise, such as "You found some beautiful leaves" or "You found them so quickly" or "That was clever of you to carry them in your shirt" or whatever seems appropriate. Lay the objects out as a display as he brings them to you to show that his work has value. (It's not just a way to relax while he runs around! Please!)

If your new learner brings you the wrong amount, don't mention it. Just count out the amount you requested and put the rest in another pile. Call that pile the "Pile of Extras" so that it still has some status.

Then add the next challenge. "Can you bring me three sticks?" Pick the kinds of things kids like, such as rocks, flowers, grass, or whatever is around your place that he might like to gather.

Add the element of color recognition, as in "Bring me one yellow flower and one red one."

Rita says she likes to throw in impossible assignments, such as "Bring me ten motorcycles," because young children enjoy telling parents or teachers when their requests are silly!

You can feel kind of righteous about this game because you are helping the little one get a chance to practice his counting and understand that each number actually stands for a unit.

If you take all the objects that were gathered and lay them out in an interesting pattern together, you've added the elements of imagination and creativity into the mix.

And you still didn't have to move (grin).

Beanbag Games

Beanbags can be easily purchased or made out of socks partly filled with dried beans or rice. Having four to six beanbags works for all the games that follow. Beanbags or socks of different colors can be used in "Throw into

Colored Container" (Game 8). Beanbags that look like frogs and other critters can be purchased to add exciting novelty.

These games could instead be played with milk or juice cartons that have been rinsed out. The cartons can be wrapped in colored paper for color matching or just to add a splash of color to the games. If you use cartons, "Balance Walk" (Game 6) has kids stepping right on the cartons. The kids will enjoy squishing the cartons, and the movement of walking on squished cartons adds an additional balance challenge.

Mats or just pieces of paper can be used in the games to indicate where the players should stand to begin the game.

What Is Being Learned

The following skills are being reinforced in these games.

SENSORY SKILLS

Vestibular feedback: One's balance is always being challenged while jumping, hopping, and leaping. Almost all the games in this series, whether they involve jumping over one beanbag or leaping over them all, stimulate vestibular awareness. When walking directly on the beanbags or cartons, one's balance is challenged further.

Proprioceptive feedback: Moving one's body to jump sideways or backward requires motor control, which stimulates muscle awareness and muscle memory. When the children throw the beanbags in the target containers at the end of the series of games, they get experience in coordinating their vision with their movement. And you get the beanbags put away!

Spatial awareness: The "In and Out" game in this series, like the one in the Plastic Bottle Games, requires the child to be aware of direction and space as she weaves in and out around the beanbags.

MOTOR SKILLS

Timing: The ability to run and leap at just the right moment takes body awareness and a sense of timing.

SOCIAL SKILLS

Taking turns: As in other games, children need to learn how to wait for their turn. Not an easy lesson. Turn taking is a difficult concept for little ones used to having all the turns or not yet aware that others also want turns. In school they come to learn that they are one of many and everyone will get a turn, just as they experience with siblings at home.

Awareness of others: When taking turns leaping over the beanbags, children need to be aware of when it is their turn to go if they are to avoid banging into the person ahead of them.

Cognitive abilities: Naming the colors of the beanbags or covered cartons adds to children's awareness of color names.

Game 1: Jump

SETUP

Lay the beanbags in a straight line with spaces in between them.

DIRECTIONS

Ask the children to jump over each beanbag. The jumper can say the name of the color jumped over, all the kids can say the names of the colors together, or there can be a combination of both.

VIDEO

http://gameslady.com/video/beanbaggames/1jumps.asp

Game 2: Jump Sideways

SETUP

Setup is the same as in the previous game.

DIRECTIONS

Ask children to jump sideways over the first beanbag leading with the left leg, and then to jump over all the other beanbags. Next ask them to turn around leading with the right leg and jump over each beanbag. For additional stimulation to their proprioceptive system, ask the children to try jumping backward.

VIDEO

http://gameslady.com/video/beanbaggames/2jump-sideways.asp

Game 3: In and Out

SETUP

Place the beanbags in a straight line or a wide oval with large spaces in between them. The spaces need to be wide enough for a child to be able to walk between the beanbags.

DIRECTIONS

Demonstrate or have one of the children demonstrate the skill of weaving in and out around the beanbags. Sing or chant words to go with the movements and encourage the rest of the class to do the same.

VIDEO

http://gameslady.com/video/beanbaggames/3-s-in-andout.asp

Game 4: Jump One, Jump Five

SETUP

Lay a mat down to mark the beginning of the jump. Lay one beanbag (or carton) down for the children to jump over, and have more beanbags ready to increase the challenge.

DIRECTIONS

Have the children line up and take turns jumping over the first beanbag, and then returning to the end of the line to jump again over a higher number of beanbags. Next turn, lay down another beanbag for a total of two. Continue to add beanbags one at a time until there are five beanbags in a row, requiring an increasingly longer broad jump. When appropriate, ask children to vary their movements by jumping sideways or backward for a good motor control experience.

VARIATION

Instead of putting the beanbags in a row, pile them on top of each other. If you are using milk cartons, this can be quite an interesting challenge!

VIDEO

http://gameslady.com/video/beanbaggames/4jump-1–2–5.asp

Game 5: Run and Leap

SETUP

Put a pile of beanbags on the floor and a mat at least five feet away.

DIRECTIONS

Ask the children to run and leap over the beanbags. Keep moving the starting mat further away so they can get up a full head of steam before they leap. This will also require the skill of readjusting their timing.

VIDEO

http://gameslady.com/video/beanbaggames/5leap.asp

Game 6: Balance Walk

SETUP

Lay the beanbags next to each other. You can lay them in a straight line, but it's more interesting to lay them in a curved line so children have to adjust their balancing posture to adapt to the changes in direction.

DIRECTIONS

Ask the children to step directly on the beanbags. If you use cartons, the children who make the cartons squish by walking on them will have their balance challenged. But so will the ones who have to keep their balance while walking on squished cartons!

Game 7: Musical Beanbags

SETUP

Give each person in the group a beanbag. Then take one beanbag away. If there are two people playing, there is only one beanbag. If there are eight, only use seven beanbags.

DIRECTIONS

Sing a phrase of a familiar song, such as "Twinkle, Twinkle, Little Star" or "Row, Row, Row Your Boat."

While the children are singing, they are also passing the beanbags from hand to hand around the circle. When the song stops, the person without a beanbag has to do something.

What that something is depends on the age level. The simplest option might be to make a silly face or jump, or the child might say the name of another child in the group and they would make a silly face together. Then, everyone imitates them. Or the person without the beanbag could be given a cognitive task, such as saying the name of a type of flower or means of transportation.

Game 8: Throw into Colored Container

SETUP

Put a mat down to show where the thrower will stand. Place a few containers into which the beanbags will be thrown a few feet in front of the mat. Use containers of different colors, or paste a piece of colored paper on each container. You will need to make some containers out of boxes or just use different colored bowls.

DIRECTIONS

Ask players to throw the red beanbags into the red container, the blue ones into the blue container, and so on. Vary the distance the container is from the mat to make the throwing tasks increasingly harder. Also, decide whether the thrower has to use the right or left hand or both hands together.

Blanket Games

You might think that walking into a classroom or therapy center with a lightweight blanket would mean that you are ready to encourage sedentary, even lying down games, but you would be wrong.

In my book *Early Intervention Games*, I mention using a blanket for a balance and strengthening game. In that game children are sitting on the blanket while others pull them around the room (or only one child could be on the blanket). That blanket game is a fun way for those who are sitting to challenge their upper body balance, and for the ones who are pulling to strengthen their upper body.

In this book, the simple material of a blanket—and just a large piece of any strong material would do—also evokes fun and encourages the development of motor, social, and sensory skills. For example, wrap a blanket tightly around two people and ask them to jump together, and they work on balance, timing, and shared attention—and they definitely gain social awareness of the other person who is snuggled up next to them!

What Is Being Learned

The following skills are being reinforced in these games.

SENSORY SKILLS

Vestibular feedback: The activity challenges children's ability to stay balanced and to pay attention to the information in their inner ear that helps them maintain an upright position.

Proprioceptive feedback: The snugness of the blanket wrapped around them makes them aware of their body, satisfies their need for being held, and helps them stay in the present moment. Moving forward while snug in a blanket or attached to a friend also requires motor planning and body awareness.

MOTOR SKILLS

Rhythm and timing: Children get an opportunity to be in sync with another person by matching their rhythm and timing. (These games will still work even if the children aren't in rhythm, but with practice this can be easily and satisfyingly learned.) Being in sync with another person also enhances social skills.

SOCIAL SKILLS

Awareness of others: Some of these games start off as individual activities and progress to having two or more children wrapped together. Children notice the difference and become very aware of their classmates and the social pleasure of connecting with another without language.

Taking turns: Waiting for one's turn and understanding that other people get a turn are important and needed concepts for children.

Setup for All the Blanket Games

1. Set up a chair for each child. Having a seat makes it easier for children to contain their excitement. Explain that every child not only will get a turn but also will get more than one turn. Expect to have to remind children to stay seated when they get eager to be next, using such comments as "Jilly is sitting quietly, so she gets to go next."

2. In the games in which the children walk wrapped in the blanket, put two pieces of paper or mats on the floor. One is the "Starting Spot" on which children stand when getting wrapped in the blanket. The other is the "Turning Spot" about ten feet away. This is the spot to which the children will walk, and at which they will then turn and return to the start.

Game 1: Sausage Walk

DIRECTIONS

For the first round, wrap a child tightly in a blanket and ask him to walk from the Starting Spot to the Turning Spot ten (or more) feet away. When he reaches the Turning Spot, help him turn around and then have him jump back to the original spot.

For the second round, wrap two children together and have them perform the same movements. They first walk to the designated spot and then turn around and jump together back to the original spot.

Children can stand beside each other, or one child can stand behind the other.

VIDEO

http://gameslady.com/video/blanketgames/1-sausage-side-side.asp

Game 2: Fat Sausage Walk

DIRECTIONS

Choose two or more children to stand together in a line, with one person in front and the others behind. The decision about how many children stand together can depend on the coordination of the children involved

or everyone's ability to handle the conse-
quences of all falling down. Children often
think falling is the "funniest" part. Wrap
the children together in the blanket. As in
the previous game, children walk forward
to the Turning Spot and then, with help,
turn around and jump back.

VIDEO

http://gameslady.com/video/
blanketgames/2-fat-sausage.asp

Game 3: Dragon

DIRECTIONS

Choose four or more children to stand together in a line, with one person
in front and the others behind that person. The children wrap their arms
around the person in front of them. Lay the blanket over all the children
except the child at the front of the line. Tell them that they are a dragon and
only the head of the dragon can see where they are going. This person, the
one who can see, then walks to a designated spot, and all the others, because
they are all holding on to each other, walk with her.

VARIATION

Have the lead person walk wherever she wants around the room (or just
in a designated area). You can stop the "dragon" at any point and ask the
children who are under the blanket if they can guess where they are in
the room. Near the door? Near the bookshelves? This aspect of the game
challenges their internal sense of where they are in space.

VIDEO

http://gameslady.com/video/blanketgames/3-dragon.asp

Game 4: Rock and Roll

DIRECTIONS

Two adults are needed. The blanket is folded in half. Each adult holds one end of the blanket. The child lies down on the blanket as if it were a hammock. The adults pick up the blanket and rock her back and forth, chanting these words:

> Rock and rock and rock and rock
> Rock and rock and roll

At the end of the chant and on the word "roll," the adults tilt the blanket close to the floor and let the child roll out. Be sure that you have a soft floor covering for this game and the next, such as carpeting or a mat.

VIDEO

http://gameslady.com/video/blanketgames/4-rock-roll.asp

Game 5: Sushi or Burrito

DIRECTIONS

Lay the blanket on the floor and have one child lie down so that his body is parallel to the bottom edge of the blanket. Then you, with the help of other children, roll the child up in the blanket as if rolling up a sushi or burrito. Once the child is rolled up, the other children pretend to eat the yummy treat.

Afterward, the edge of the blanket is lifted up, and the child is carefully or quickly unrolled depending on his sensibilities. Again, as in the previous game, you might want to have a soft floor covering, such as carpeting or a mat. If that's not available, unroll slowly.

VIDEO

http://gameslady.com/video/blanketgames/5-a-sushi.asp

Game 6: Trampoline

DIRECTIONS

Lay the blanket out flat and have each child pick up an edge until everyone is standing around the blanket, holding it at waist level. Place a ball or stuffed toy or doll in the center of the blanket and help the children learn to bounce the object up and down by lifting and lowering the blanket. With practice, the children learn that if they all lift and lower at the same time—that is, work together—they can have more control over how long the object is bounced before it rolls off the blanket.

VIDEO

http://gameslady.com/video/blanketgames/6-trampoline.asp

Game 7: Dance Around

DIRECTIONS

As in the previous game, this game starts with all the children holding on to the edge of the blanket. Put on any music and let the kids dance around in a circle. At the end of the song, they all lift the blanket and go underneath. The end.

VIDEO

http://gameslady.com/video/blanketgames/7-dance-around.asp

Two-by-Four Games

All that is required for this series of games is some simple wooden boards; a few sand- or bean-filled socks; and some small step stools, if you want, to increase the balance challenge. The series of games uses four pieces of two-by four-inch pieces of lumber that are around four feet long, and starts with motor activities that can lead to a cognitive game called "Going to the Store." Objects for the store game are just the usual grocery items you buy or any small objects.

Ideally, you gather the materials listed here. If you only have one simple two-by-four, you can still play most of the games. Instead of going around the boards, in the first game, children just jump off at the end and walk back to the beginning.

The filled socks, whether filled with sand or beans, are used in a couple of ways to increase a child's balancing skills. When placed on top of the two-by-fours they add an obstacle to step over, and when placed under the two-by-fours they make the boards tilt from side to side.

These boards can also be set up as in Game 1, "How Many Ways." The setup can be left up in a corner of the bedroom or classroom, and the kids can play at different times of the day.

Materials

- Four two-by-fours that are four (more or less) feet long
- Two small step stools
- Two or more socks that have been filled with sand or rice or other dried legumes

- Grocery items or any small objects
- A table
- A tray (optional)

Note: Two of the boards could be wider, such as two inches by six inches, and around four feet long, if you want to have some beams that are easier to balance on. The wider the board, the easier it is to walk on.

What Is Being Learned

The following skills are being reinforced in these games.

SENSORY SKILLS

Vestibular feedback: These games are all about balance and the vestibular system that controls balance. Walking on a two-by-four while it is moving (as in Game 3, "Crossing the Seesaw Beam") is the ultimate balance challenge in this series.

Tactile feedback: Children need to feel the board with their feet to give them extra clues about walking in that narrow space.

MOTOR SKILLS

Eye-foot coordination: Walking on a balance beam while stepping over filled socks provides an experience in balance and eye-foot coordination.

Agility and strength: Jumping off the ends of the boards and jumping over the boards give practice in strength, agility, and timing.

SOCIAL SKILLS

Learning together: Game 6, "Going to the Store," in particular provides many opportunities to learn colors, shapes, phonics, and even rhyming.

Awareness of others: Walking with others around the boards while all doing the same thing, such as having their hands on their head, produces a feeling of being together and being silly with others.

Game 1: How Many Ways Can You Walk on the Beams?

SETUP

Place the four boards in a rectangular shape.

DIRECTIONS

Children walk around the boards, maintaining their balance while following different commands, such as

1. Walk forward with one hand on your head.
2. Walk forward with your arms straight up above your head.
3. Walk forward with your arms crossed.
4. Walk sideways with your arms on your hips and your right leg leading.
5. Walk sideways with your arms on your hips and your left leg leading.
6. Walk backward with your arms out to your sides, like a tightrope walker.
7. Walk on tiptoe.
8. Walk in a tight heel-toe pattern, placing the heel of the foot directly in front and touching the toe of the other foot.
9. Walk while balancing an object on your head.
10. Walk showing different emotions. Walk like you're mad. Walk like you're sad (and so on).

11. Walk together in a line with your hands on the shoulders of the person in front of you. (This is a useful variation with children who have some difficulty balancing on their own. Pair them with someone who has stronger balancing skills, or have three children walk together and place the child with the weakest balancing ability in the middle.)

Everyone can also get a turn making up a way for others to walk on the beams.

Game 2: Frogs on the Beam

SETUP

Fill socks with sand or beans and place them on the two-by-fours. If you draw faces on the socks, you can call them frogs.

DIRECTIONS

Have children step over the sand-filled "frogs" on the beams. They could also be given an empty tray, pick up each frog, and carry the tray to the end. (Using a tray adds an extra challenge to the activity because children can't see their feet and must rely totally on their vestibular system for balance and tactile system for feeling the board with their feet.)

Game 3: Crossing the Seesaw Beam

SETUP

Place socks that have been filled with sand or rice or other dried legumes under the middle of a board. If you don't have socks, try using a hard pillow or even a small wood block.

DIRECTIONS

As children start at one end of the board, the board will tilt as if they are walking on a ramp. When they get to the middle of the board, the weight will shift and the board will tilt the opposite way. Children are encouraged to maintain their balance while the board moves. Children can also stand in the middle of the board and rock it from side to side.

Note: If I know a child might have difficulty, I stand casually near the center or tipping point of the board. This way, a child can reach out and use me to maintain balance without looking like she is asking for help.

Game 4: Little Jump, Big Jump, Little Jump

SETUP

Place the four boards horizontally on the floor. The first board is placed by itself, the next two boards are close together, and the fourth board is by itself.

DIRECTIONS

Children are facing the horizontal boards; they jump forward over the first board (little jump), then jump over the set of two boards (big jump), and then jump over the last single board (little jump). If you want, you can make the two boards wider apart to make an even bigger jump.

Children can also hop over the boards and jump backward and sideways.

Children can take turns and jump one at a time. They can also hold hands and jump in teams of two or more.

Game 5: Hop to the End

SETUP

Instead of horizontally, two boards are placed parallel to each other. A board is placed perpendicular to those boards at one end.

DIRECTIONS

Children hop on one foot between the two boards and then jump over the end board. Ask the children to hop first on the left foot and then on the right.

Game 6: Going to the Store

SETUP

Place a board perpendicular to a table. You can have the board on the floor or raised on stools or placed on something uneven, such as sand-filled socks or pillows. On the table, place a group of common grocery containers, such as empty cereal boxes, juice bottles, yogurt tubs, and so on. You could also use any objects, especially miniatures.

DIRECTIONS

An adult plays the role of "Mother" or "Father," who tells the children, one by one, what they each need to get at the store. You can play this with a group of children, taking turns, or with just one child who gets to have every turn! The child is given a tray and told to cross the "bridge" (a board) and go to the "store" (the table at the end of the board), and bring back something, for example, that . . .

◆   Starts with a certain sound

◆   Starts with a certain letter

◆   Is a certain color

◆   Has a certain function or movement

◆   Rhymes with a certain word

By having a variety of possible clues, children with different cognitive levels can all play together and all can be successful at their task.

For example, a milk carton could be. . .

◆   Something that starts with the letter *M*

◆   Something that starts with the sound "mmmm"

◆   Something that has white liquid inside or is in a box with red (or another color) on it

◆   Something that makes our bones stronger

◆   Something that rhymes with "silk"

Game 7: Make Up Your Own

SETUP

Let any child who is interested have an opportunity to arrange the boards any way he or she wants that looks safe to you. Some teachers like to leave the boards in a specific place in the classroom so children can play the games on their own whenever they wish.

DIRECTIONS

The child who arranged the boards gets to say how it is to be walked, jumped, or hopped.

Hula-Hoop Games

Hula-Hoops were a big craze during my adolescent years, and if you were cool, you could make it go round and round on your hips ad infinitum.

I know now that there are a lot more things to do with Hula-Hoops. If you're a performer, you can keep it going around every limb and your neck at the same time. But if you are a kid, there are even "funner" games to play. Children can crawl through them, jump inside them, roll them, kick them, and many other possibilities. Games 1 to 6 can be played sequentially with slight modifications in the positioning of the hoops.

Here are twelve variations on games using hoops, and, oh yeah, one involves the traditional way of Hula-Hooping, only faster.

What Is Being Learned

The following skills are being reinforced in these games.

SENSORY SKILLS

Vestibular feedback: The vestibular system is stimulated in many of these games, as children need to keep their balance while tiptoeing, kicking, jumping, and hopping. In Game 1, "Tiptoe Through the Hoops," for example, the vestibular system is engaged as children become aware of lifting one leg high enough or stand on their toes to maneuver their way through the hoops without stepping on them. In Game 9, "Roll and Kick," kicking the hoop with the side of one's foot requires keeping one's balance intact.

Proprioceptive feedback: Many games in this series encourage awareness of body movement. In Game 7, "Roll the Hoop," and Game 8, "Boomerang," for example, knowing where to place one hand and roll with the other is necessary to maintain control over the direction of the roll. A successful roll aimed in just the right direction is the indicator that you got it right.

MOTOR SKILLS

Timing: Being able to kick the hoop at just the right moment and catch it as it comes flying through the air encourages this awareness.

Strength: There are so many ways of laying out the hoops for a jumping and hopping game that it will be easy to build leg strength.

SOCIAL SKILLS

Awareness of others: In Game 7, "Roll the Hoop," in which children work with partners, they need to be aware of each other and aim their hoop in the correct direction to make it easy for their partner to catch the hoop and roll it back. Group games also encourage awareness of others because one child is behind another, and if children aren't spatially aware, traffic jams and pileups may result.

Social support: Children who are too shy to jump through a maze on their own can be paired with another child, and they can do it together.

Game 1: Tiptoe Through the Hoops

SETUP

This game can be done in two ways. In the easier version, the hoops are laid on the ground, each hoop overlapping the other. In the harder version, adults hold the hoops horizontally about four inches off the ground. It helps to have a person to direct the traffic so that after children have tiptoed through the maze, they leave the last hoop and walk back to the first hoop to begin again.

DIRECTIONS

Ask the children to tiptoe from the first hoop to the last by walking in the empty spaces. Ask them to try not to step on the hoop itself. You can add a bit of extra fun by pretending the hoops are made of ice, and if these round icicles are stepped on, you'd get some popsicle toes!

In the harder version, when the hoops are raised above ground level, children will need to lift each foot high to go over the hoop and get into each empty space.

If you know the song "Tiptoe Through the Tulips," sing it or any other ditty that fits the movements.

Game 2: Crawl Tunnel

SETUP

The hoops are now held vertically to form a tunnel, with the hoops touching the floor. Two or more people can hold the hoops. The more people and hoops, the longer the tunnel will be. One or two hoops can be raised above the others to make a section that needs to be crawled over to encourage changes in body awareness and motor control.

DIRECTIONS

Children crawl through the tunnel. Remind the kids that traffic goes one way so they do not turn around at the end of the tunnel and head back through. Some children emerging from the tunnel may need guidance to return to the beginning to help them stay on task.

VIDEO

http://gameslady.com/video/hoopgames/2-tunnel.asp

Game 3: Jumping Maze

SETUP

There is such a wide variety of ways to set up the hoops to enhance jumping and hopping skills.

Here are possibilities:

- *Straight line*: This is the simplest and can accommodate a large variety of movements.
- *Hopscotch pattern*: This pattern encourages alternating from jumping on two feet to hopping on one.
- *Circle*: This pattern lets everyone play at the same time without waiting for a turn.
- *Wavy line*: This pattern allows for awareness of subtle changes in direction.
- *Box shape*: This pattern encourages sharp changes in movement from one direction to another.

DIRECTIONS

Have the children move through the different patterns according to the directions you choose to give. Children can

- Jump directly from one hoop to another with one big jump
- Jump several times using small jumps inside each hoop to get from one hoop to another
- Hop from one hoop to another
- Jump or hop backward or sideways
- Jump and twirl their body in a circle from one hoop to land in another
- March forward or backward from hoop to hoop

You can also let children make up directions for others to follow.

Game 4: Combination—Vertical and Horizontal

SETUP

Decide which skills you want to work on and set up a combination of hoops accordingly. For example, you might want to combine jumping skills with the more precise balancing required by tiptoeing. Or perhaps you want the children to change levels and go from jumping to tunnel crawling. Changing levels requires more body awareness as the child stoops low enough to go through. Overlapping horizontal hoops encourage tiptoeing and balance. Hoops held vertically and low encourage crawling and spatial awareness. Hoops on the floor in any of the patterns listed earlier in "Jumping Maze" encourage jumping and hopping and body awareness.

This is a turn-taking game in which each child does it alone and the others wait until that child has completed the set before the next one goes.

DIRECTIONS

Decide on the movements wanted, and give directions accordingly. Explain the sequence of movements using prepositional phrases, such as "jumping over," "going through," "going under," and so on. Children can take turns setting up the course and holding the upright hoops.

Game 5: Backward

SETUP

Set up one of the different combinations from Game 4.

DIRECTIONS

Have the children do the previous game backward. Going backward is a bigger challenge, as it requires children to have a spatial sense of where things are behind them.

Game 6: All Together Now

SETUP

Use any combination from Game 4.

DIRECTIONS

This is the no-waiting way, whereby children can go directly behind one another. This is good to do after everyone has had a solo turn or two, and it changes the energy from individual waiting to everybody going. This is also a good method if a child is too shy to do it alone; he can go with a buddy.

Game 7: Roll the Hoop

SETUP

Rolling the hoop takes a moment or two of demonstration to show the correct technique. Some children may need a hand-over-hand approach to get the feel of the correct hand positioning. Basically, the hoop is held vertically, with the bottom touching the floor. One hand is open and flat against the top of the hoop holding it steady, with palm down. The second hand is at the back of the hoop and pushes it forward.

DIRECTIONS

Have two children, such as siblings, neighborhood kids, or classmates, be partners and, at first, stand near each other (say about two feet apart). One child rolls the hoop to the other, and then the other rolls it back. Once they get the idea, they can enlarge the distance between them. If you wanted all the kids to play together or only have a couple of hoops for the group, form a circle, and players can roll the hoop to the player across the circle or just to the one next to them.

VIDEO

http://gameslady.com/video/hoopgames/7-roll-to-each-other.asp

Game 8: Boomerang

SETUP

In this individual game, the technique is the same as when rolling the hoop, except instead of the hoop rolling to another, it boomerangs back. The child holds the hoop vertically with one hand on top and the other on the backside.

DIRECTIONS

Instead of just rolling it forward, the child gives the hoop a bit of a backward pull first. The hoop will roll forward and then boomerang back.

VIDEO

http://gameslady.com/video/hoopgames/8—boomerang.asp

Game 9: Roll and Kick

SETUP

Two children stand about five feet apart. One child is the "Roller," and the other is the "Kicker."

DIRECTIONS

The Roller rolls the hoop to the Kicker. The Kicker kicks the lower part of the hoop using the side of his foot. The hoop flies in the air, and the Roller catches it.

Game 10: Ring Toss

SETUP

Stand any object to toss the hoop over. It can be a small chair, a traffic cone, or even a person with her arms held firmly at her sides.

DIRECTIONS

Each child has a turn holding the hoop horizontally with both hands and tossing it over the standing object. Have children stand further and further away from the object to increase the challenge.

VIDEO

http://gameslady.com/video/hoopgames/10-toss.asp

Game 11: Jump Rope

SETUP

The player stands inside the hoop, holding it at waist level. The front of the hoop is touching the front of the player's waist. The rest of the hoop is behind her back.

DIRECTIONS

The jumper brings the hoop over her head to the front and jumps over it. The jump can be done with one leg leading or with both legs jumping.

VIDEO

http://gameslady.com/video/hoopgames/11-jump-rope.asp

Game 12: Hula-Hooping—Fast and in Circles

SETUP

The player places the hoop around his waist in the traditional way.

DIRECTIONS

The player makes the hoop go slowly around his waist, gradually increasing the speed. The player can also go around in a circle while the hoop is spinning.

VIDEO

http://gameslady.com/video/hoopgames/12-hula-.asp

Unusual Gifts That Cost a Little and Please a Lot

When my daughter Marissa was four years old, she flashed her eyes at every good-looking male and told me she wanted to grow up to be Cinderella. It wasn't what I had in mind; I was thinking more along the lines of an astrophysicist–prima ballerina. But not one to impose my expectations on others, I called a local flower shop and ordered a pink nosegay bouquet for her birthday. She was thrilled and put on the lacy white slip she called her Cinderella dress and all her costume jewelry, and with her nosegay looked, I admit, like a fairy princess.

I'm telling you this in case you have a Cinderella of your own and need an idea for a gift.

Finding the right gift can be wearing. I find it easier if I think of something ahead of time rather than wander around a store and end up buying something expensive that's still not right.

So, if you want ideas, here are some inexpensive gifts for children that I have tried that went over well:

- *Colored ribbon*: Get a large assortment of ribbon, with about a yard of each color. Include different textures, such as satin, velvet, and woven. Get a floral tin to put them in.

- *Business supplies*: Buy such items as paper clips, staplers, hole punchers, folding files, index cards (with their box), a ledger, tape, rulers, a receipt book with carbon, a stamp pad, and stamps. You can get an empty boot box to sort them in. These supplies will keep kids busy for hours, and isn't that what busi-ness is all about anyway?

- *Cotton*: A box of cotton or cotton balls can make a great gift. Kids sometimes just like to plunge their hands into all that softness or use cotton to stuff small pillows or paste it on pictures to make clouds and beards.

- *An all-purpose cape*: If you are good at sewing, make a cape out of velvet or glossy satin or some other spectacular material so your child can be a super-person or prince or sorceress. If you don't sew, secondhand stores are good for finding dramatic clothes and gobs of gaudy costume jewelry.

- *Shoe box art*: Most shoe stores will give you all the shoe boxes you could ever want if you ask them to save some for you. They make wonderful trains for the younger child: connect them with a piece of string, leaving a long piece at the front for pull-ing. You can add wheels, paint, animals, and so on. Larger boot boxes can be deco-rated and personalized to make a private place for your child's "treasures."

- *Magnifying glass*: I once read somewhere that "no self-respecting five-year-old should be without a magnifying glass." I took that sentiment to heart, and by add-ing a string of yarn made a small magnifying glass into a necklace for my then

five-year-old. She wore it constantly for weeks and weeks, checking out the whole world, up close and personal.

- ◆ *A ream of paper and a package of pens*: I can't imagine that there is an up-and-coming artist, writer, or scribbler alive who wouldn't love five hundred sheets of paper all her own!

- ◆ *Books*: Always books. It's impossible to overestimate the importance of books in a child's development. A man named Strickland Gillilan said it well:

> You may have tangible wealth untold;
> Caskets of jewels and coffers of gold.
> Richer than I you can never be—
> I had a Mother who read to me.

Ladder Games

In these games, I used a bamboo ladder I found at a store selling home decorations. I think it was meant to hang towels on. I'm not suggesting that a bamboo ladder is easy to find, although a section of an extension ladder could also be used. I also used mats or pieces of paper to mark where the player would stand to begin the game.

I'm including this decorative ladder as a possibility for a variety of games to make the point that almost anything can be used to develop motor, sensory, and social awareness. I brought the ladder to school one day, laid it on the ground, and had the children do the obvious basic motor skills. They jumped from one space to the next. They hopped on one foot. They tiptoed. They jumped to every other space. They walked on the rungs to challenge their balance, and they walked with a foot on either side of the ladder.

I thought that I had come up with every possible idea.

Then I let the children take turns coming up with their own ideas. I was surprised. They had many, and they were original and perfect. For example, one girl turned the ladder on its side and called up certain friends one by one (she was the teacher now!) to straddle the ladder with her. Then, together they rocked it from side to side, making this game one that really stimulated the vestibular system! Another game required that the children jump over the ladder going from one side to the other. Another child chose to alternate jumping with two feet inside the space to jumping with both feet outside the ladder, bringing the adductor and abductor muscles into the game.

Surely, I thought, there couldn't be any more ways to play on a ladder.

Later, I found I was wrong again.

I walked into the afternoon class. The teacher was using the ladder to play games, and she had come up with more variations. One was to place the ladder on its side and have children crawl through the spaces. She added imagination by having them pretend the ladder was hot and if they touched it they would get burned to make them more conscious of their movements. My favorite was asking six children to stand in the spaces of the ladder and then lean down and pull the ladder to waist level. Then she had the kids walk forward and backward together and then make a complete circle, all working and walking together. What a wonderful way to work on being aware of others, I thought. I was impressed and told her so.

"Those are very creative ideas," I said. She looked surprised. She said, "But . . . I knew you were doing games with the ladder this morning, and I thought these were what you were doing!"

Just shows, everyone has ideas, and they all can work!

What Is Being Learned

The following skills are being reinforced in these games.

SENSORY SKILLS

Vestibular feedback: One's balance is being challenged while jumping, hopping, and tiptoeing, especially when the space is limited to the area between the rungs. Walking on the sides of the ladder also takes balancing.

Proprioceptive feedback: Being aware of how to move one's body to accomplish the different tasks takes body awareness.

Spatial awareness: Getting through the spaces without touching the sides requires an awareness of where one's body parts are for each part of the move.

MOTOR SKILLS

Motor planning: Jumping from one end of the ladder to the other in two, three, or four jumps takes an awareness of how to plan the movement to do it.

Rhythm: Imitating the patterned sequences of using two, three, or four jumps stimulates rhythmic sense.

SOCIAL SKILLS

Taking turns: As in other games, children need to learn to wait patiently for their turn.

Awareness of others: When straddling the ladder or standing between the rungs, children get a chance to work together with others to make the ladder move.

Creativity: Getting an opportunity to imagine other possibilities, such as jumping while tapping one's head and rubbing one's stomach or while humming a tune, encourages thinking outside the box!

Game 1: Jump Between the Rungs

SETUP

Lay the ladder on the floor. Place a mat at one end to mark the beginning and another at the other end.

DIRECTIONS

Ask the children to start at the beginning and jump from one space to the next from one end of the ladder to the other. Next ask the children to jump to every other space or every third space. Can they go from one end to the other in three jumps? Two? One? Can they jump backward?

VIDEOS

http://gameslady.com/video/laddergames/1-ladder-jump.asp
http://gameslady.com/video/laddergames/3-ladder-backward.asp

Game 2: Hop Between the Rungs

SETUP

Lay the ladder and the mats on the floor as in Game 1.

DIRECTIONS

Have children hop first on their right foot and then on their left between each rung from one end to the other.

VIDEO

http://gameslady.com/video/laddergames/2-ladder-hopping.asp

Game 3: Tiptoe Between the Rungs

SETUP

Lay the ladder and mats on the floor as in the previous games.

DIRECTIONS

Have the children tiptoe from space to space. Next, change it to have them walk on their heels.

VIDEO

http://gameslady.com/video/laddergames/4-ladder-tip-toe.asp

Game 4: Walk on the Rungs

SETUP

Lay the ladder and mats on the floor as in the previous games.

DIRECTIONS

Have children walk on the rungs from one end to the other. They can go forward or backward. You can make it more exciting by pretending the children are performers in a circus and you are doing the commentary, as in "Julien will now attempt to walk on the rungs. He is starting! He has done half of them, ladies and gentlemen, without falling! He did it! Amazing!"

VIDEO

http://gameslady.com/video/laddergames/7-ladder-rungs.asp

Game 5: Jump In and Out

SETUP

Lay the ladder and mats on the floor as in the previous games.

DIRECTIONS

Have children jump with feet together in the space between the rungs and then alternate with a jump with both feet on either side of the ladder. They continue jumping from one end to the other.

VIDEO

http://gameslady.com/video/laddergames/9-ladder-jump-in-and-out.asp

Game 6: Go Through the Window

SETUP

Turn the ladder on its side and have an adult or another child hold it.

DIRECTIONS

Have each child crawl through the spaces between the rungs. You can add to their imagination and careful movements by pretending the ladder is hot and they have to keep their body from touching the ladder and getting "burned." If a child takes your words literally, you might need to explain that this is just "pretend" and let him feel the ladder to be sure.

Two or more children can do this at the same time, or one child can do it by starting at one end of the ladder and weaving in and out of the spaces until she reaches the end of the ladder.

VIDEO

http://gameslady.com/video/laddergames/5-ladder-thru-window.asp

Game 7: Rock the Boat

SETUP

Hold the ladder on its side, as in the previous game.

DIRECTIONS

Have children straddle the ladder, with everyone getting on and rocking it from side to side. Their feet touch the ground, and they work together, leaning from one side to the other. They can sing "Row, Row, Row Your Boat" or other tunes to help coordinate the movements.

VIDEO

http://gameslady.com/video/laddergames/12-rock-the-boat.asp

Game 8: Working Together

SETUP

Lay the ladder flat on the floor.

DIRECTIONS

Have kids stand in the spaces between the rungs, one child in each space.

Then have them reach down and pick up the ladder and walk together backward, forward, and in a circle.

VIDEO

http://gameslady.com/video/laddergames/13-ladder-circles.asp

Game 9: Rhythm

SETUP

Lay the ladder flat on the floor.

DIRECTIONS

Demonstrate a rhythmic movement, such as jumping three times in the first three spaces of the ladder and then hopping on one foot in the last two. The children can each make up their own rhythm for others to imitate.

VIDEO

http://gameslady.com/video/laddergames/15-ladder-rhythm.asp

Game 10: Creating New Games

SETUP

Each child gets to decide.

DIRECTIONS

Children can make up whatever movements they want to do with the ladder or with any objects you find or have at home or in the classroom. Players can do their movements by themselves or invite others to participate. Maybe it could be a birthday party game of "do your own thing."

VIDEO

http://gameslady.com/video/laddergames/14-ladder-creative.asp

Magazine Tube Games

Magazines, with their high-gloss, colorful ads, seem too nice to just toss away without reusing. In these games, two or more pages rolled up into a tube make a very nifty object, whether you are playing with your family or your class. Just having the kids roll the pages up and tape them closed is already a good fine motor task. The resulting tubes can be played with in a variety of ways. Using them as mini-swords might come first to a little boy's mind (if you think that is a biased statement, you don't work with little boys), but with your clever guidance, you can show them all the other things that can be done that are just as fun.

Because there are so many possibilities, you can have a lot of control. If the kids are getting too noisy when they are playing the flute game, add some rhythm taps to modify the action or change it to a tossing or jumping game. You can decide how quickly to go from one variation to another by noticing the energy of the moment. If they have been sitting in a circle practicing their eye-hand coordination for a while and start to get fidgety, change the game to a parade in which they get to walk and "play" their flute at the same time.

What Is Being Learned

The following skills are being reinforced in these games.

SENSORY SKILLS

Vestibular feedback: Not much balancing is required in the parts in which everyone sits in a circle. But once they are up and jumping over ever widening "creeks," the vestibular system is engaged!

MOTOR SKILLS

Eye-hand coordination: Throwing and catching always involve watching what is being thrown and knowing where your hands are. Are they in position to catch the object? This takes knowing where one's body is and attending to what one's hand are doing.

Timing: Throwing tubes in the air and getting your hand in just the right spot at just the right time take, along with eye-hand coordination, a sense of timing.

SOCIAL SKILLS

Awareness of self: Playing throwing games, which some of these are, takes focus and attention so you don't miss the catch.

Feeling part of the group: No waiting for a turn for most of these games—everyone is trying at the same time. When the tube game becomes a jumping, imagination, or rhythm game, children get the social experience of being aware of others and taking turns.

Cognitive abilities: You can add a cognitive component during the throwing games. Ask the child to throw at a named object—such as something that is square, a specific letter, or a color on the wall. While sitting and tossing the tube, you can ask the children to count how many times they can throw and catch.

Creativity: Children can take turns coming up with creative answers in the game "What Else Can It Be?" A magazine tube could be a comb or telescope.

Setup for All the Magazine Tube Games

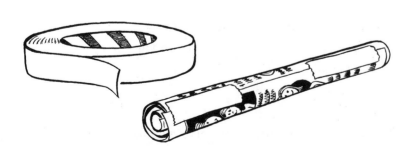

You will need some old magazines and masking tape. Have each child tear two or three pages from one of the magazines and roll them into a tube. Use masking tape to hold the tube shut. Some children will need to have the rolling started for them so the tube will be tight. Tear off the right-size piece of tape for children who need help taping the tube shut.

VIDEO

http://gameslady.com/video/magtube/1-make-own-tube.asp

Game 1: Flute

DIRECTIONS

Show the children how to hum through the tubes to make sounds. You can let children just make whatever sounds they want, or you can start a familiar tune, such as "Twinkle, Twinkle, Little Star." You can combine flute playing with rhythm by alternately blowing into the tube and then hitting the tube on the floor to establish a rhythm. You can have everyone stand up and walk around the room in a Pied Piper fashion, humming away on their respective flutes. If you want, even add some movements, such as jumping or twirling.

VIDEO

http://gameslady.com/video/magtube/2-tube-flute-copy.asp

Game 2: Easy Throw

DIRECTIONS

Have children hold their tube in both hands, palms up. Demonstrate how to gently toss the tube up with both hands. Encourage the players to start with small tosses before increasing the distance. Once your players gain confidence in their ability to throw and catch and can increase the distance thrown, add the twirl. Show the players how to turn their wrist as they throw the tube so that it twirls in the air. Encourage your players to keep their eyes on the tube as it twirls in the air so that they will have their hands in the right place to catch it.

How high can they twirl and still catch the tube?

VIDEO

http://gameslady.com/video/magtube/3—tube-easy-throw.asp

Game 3: Hand to Hand

DIRECTIONS

Have children hold their tube vertically in one hand. Show them how to toss the tube from hand to hand. Start with the hands close together, and gradually enlarge the distance between the hands.

VIDEO

http://gameslady.com/video/magtube/4-tube-hand-to-hand.asp

Game 4: Reflex Drop

DIRECTIONS

Have children hold the tube up high vertically in one hand. They place the other hand directly below the first hand, preparing to catch the dropped tube. They drop the tube from the top hand and catch it with the waiting hand. Have children gradually increase the distance between the two hands.

Now switch hands. Ask, "Is one hand faster?"

VIDEO

http://gameslady.com/video/magtube/5—reflex-drop.asp

Game 5: Head Drop

DIRECTIONS

Have children place the tube horizontally on their head. Show them how to hold their hands by their chest to be ready to catch the tube, and how to tilt their head forward so the tube falls into their waiting hands.

VIDEO

http://gameslady.com/video/magtube/7-tubr-head-drop.asp

Game 6: Throw at a Target

SETUP

Look around the room for different shapes or colors or tape shapes and colors beforehand on the wall. Find or tape shapes or colors that are at and above eye level. The target could be large at first so everyone is successful. Depending on the skill levels, the targets can be progressively smaller, which would require better aim.

DIRECTIONS

Ask players to throw their tube like a javelin at the color or shape named. Do it at the count of three: "One, two, three—throw!"

VIDEO

http://gameslady.com/video/magtube/8—throw.asp

Game 7: Jump over the Tubes

SETUP

Take all the tubes from the children and lay them horizontally in a row on the floor, with one right after the other and an eight- to twelve-inch space between them.

DIRECTIONS

Have the children jump over each tube into the space behind it. Players jump over the first tube and then the second, and so on. Keep changing the method. Possibilities are to jump forward, backward, or sideways; hop on one foot; jump to every other one; jump from the first to the last; jump and twirl in a half circle before landing; jump with eyes closed and hands on head; and so on.

If one student is in a wheelchair, he could be the "boss" and tell everyone the method to use and even add different dimensions. "Charlie, you jump to every other one while humming 'Itsy Bitsy Spider.'" Or if students are in a line waiting their turn to jump, the person directly behind them can dictate the method of jumping (for example, "Sadia, you have to jump backward while rubbing your head").

VIDEO

http://gameslady.com/video/magtube/9-jump-over.asp

Game 8: What Else Can It Be?

SETUP

Children sit in a circle. There is only one tube.

DIRECTIONS

Chant these words:

"A tube, a tube, what else can it be?"

If the first child mimes an action showing it's a telescope, change the chant to:

"A telescope, a telescope, what else can it be?"

If the next child pretends it's a baton, change the words accordingly:

"A baton, a baton, what else can it be?" (and so on, until everyone has had a turn).

Game 9: We've Got a Rhythm Inside of Us

DIRECTIONS

Show children how to hold one end of a tube and tap the floor with the other end to make a sound. Players take turns tapping their tube on the floor in a variety of rhythms that everyone has to listen to and try to imitate. Every one gets a chance to be the star!

Plastic Bottle Games

At first it seemed great that so many people were drinking water instead of soda, but the excess plastic bottles have become a problem for the environment, and you are warned not to reuse them for drinking water.

Sure you could recycle them, but you could also reuse them to make a variety of great children's games. Children can bowl them down, leap over them, and weave in and out around them. And these are only some of the possibilities. Leave it to your kids to think of more!

What Is Being Learned

The following skills are being reinforced in these games.

SENSORY SKILLS

Vestibular feedback: There are elements of vestibular stimulation when one is throwing and weaving one's body between obstacles, as is done in these games.

Proprioceptive feedback: Knowing how far and high to jump to go over an obstacle takes knowing which muscles to use to accomplish the task. "Knock-Downs" and "Obstacle Course" use these learned skills.

Spatial awareness: "In and Out" is about understanding directionality and spatial awareness. Weaving in and out around the bottles takes a sense of which direction one needs to go to form this pattern of movement.

MOTOR SKILLS

Eye-hand coordination: Knowing which muscles to use to throw a ball far or fast requires body awareness.

SOCIAL SKILLS

Awareness of others: Watching others take their turn and getting the chance to cheer for them when they do well promote an awareness of one's classmates.

Taking turns: Waiting for one's turn in these games is easy, as the turns are quick. The fast pace also makes it easier to notice how others do because children can get distracted if the wait is longer.

Cognitive abilities: How many bottles are knocked down? Children are asked to notice and count.

Game 1: Knock-Downs

SETUP

Preparing the bottles: How easy or how hard it is to knock bottles down depends on two things: how close the bottles are to each other, and how heavy or light they are. To make the bottles heavier, add water, sand, or gravel. How much material will affect the weight and ease in falling over. If bottles are clear, you might want to get the children involved in adding color. Start the session by having children put drops of food coloring in the bottles (this is a good teachable moment to learn that, for example, a drop of red food coloring and a drop of yellow make orange-colored water). If you do add water, tighten the caps securely, seal with crazy glue, or wrap with tape to prevent possible leaking when the bottles are knocked down.

Preparing the site: Place a mat or piece of paper on the floor to indicate where the thrower should stand. This gives you the option of moving the mat closer or further away to make the task easier or harder. Because children get to throw the ball two times on each turn, you can move the mat closer on the second turn to increase the chances of success for the child who is less skilled. You can also move the mat further away on the second turn for the child who needs more challenge.

Choosing the ball size: The size of the ball can vary from tennis ball size to soccer ball size in the same game. Start with the larger size. Remember, when using the smaller-size ball, that it is a bit easier to knock the bottles down if they are closer together.

Arranging the bottles: When setting up the bottles, you have two options:

- Place the bottles in one long row facing the thrower. How far apart to place the bottles depends on the amount of challenge wanted. The closer the bottles are to each other, the easier they are to knock down.
- Bottles can be placed in a typical bowling pin pyramid configuration.

DIRECTIONS

Ask the child to knock the bottles down. You can demonstrate your preference for rolling the ball as in a game of bowling. Some children, not yet skilled in underhand throws, might prefer to throw the ball overhand before they understand the difference.

Have the child count how many bottles are knocked down.

VARIATIONS

1. One or two children are assigned the task of standing the bottles back up after they have been knocked down. All of the bottles are set back up after each child has had a turn.

2. The bottles knocked down stay down until everyone has had a turn. This increases the challenge for the last kids in line, as they have to aim the ball more accurately to hit the few remaining bottles.

VIDEO

http://gameslady.com/video/bottlegames/1-Bottle-throw-ball.asp

Game 2: In and Out

SETUP

Place the bottles in a wide oval or circle. The spaces between the bottles need to be wide enough for a child to be able to walk between the bottles.

DIRECTIONS

Demonstrate the skill of individually walking in and out of the circle by going around the bottles. You can use the image of a car going around the obstacles. Sing or chant words to go with the movements and encourage the rest of the class to do the same. I use words like these, sung to a simple tune:

> Go in and out the bottles
> Go in and out the bottles
> Go in and out the bottles
> All on a beautiful day

VARIATIONS

1. Have two children do it together. Invoke the image of a van rather than an individual car going in and out of the circle. This is especially useful if one child does not have the spatial understanding to do the movement on her own. The other child can be the leader, and the child with less experience can place her hands on the leader's shoulders or on his waist. You might need to widen the space between the bottles by making the circle a little bigger to accommodate the extra person.

2. When two children are going together, you can change the mental image from a van to a horse and rider by putting a rope, scarf, or ribbon around the leader's waist. The follower can hold on to the reins as the horse leads him in and out around the bottles.

3. A small train of three children can also hold on to each other and go in and out of the circle. Any more than three children, and bottles get too easily knocked over and the circle or oval pattern is lost. If you want to form a larger train and use more than three players, place the bottles in a straight line instead of in a circle or oval. Make sure there is a lot of room in between the bottles.

4. You can eventually add the challenge of body awareness by placing the bottles close enough to each other that the child has to turn his body sideways to go in and out of the circle. But, at first, make sure there is plenty of room to go around the bottles without knocking them down. When they get knocked down, they have to be put back up for the next player or players, and that takes a little time away from the flow.

VIDEO

http://gameslady.com/video/bottlegames/2-Bottle-in-out.asp

Game 3: Obstacle Course

SETUP

Place the mat (or piece of paper) down at one end of the play area to mark the start of the game. In front of the mat, lay two bottles side by side. Leave a space or mat for a player to land on after she jumps over the two bottles. Next, lay a set of three bottles down for the player to jump over. The bottles are also lying on their side, close together and touching each other. Leave a space or mat to land on. Next, stand two bottles up for the player to weave through. Lay a final mat to mark the end of the obstacle course.

DIRECTIONS

Ask the players to jump over the two sets of bottles lying on their side and to weave in and out around the others. Encourage the players to jump on the final mat.

Children can do this obstacle course one at a time with everyone clapping at the final jump. Children can also form a line and go right after each other.

VARIATIONS

1. You can change the order of the obstacle course using these same motoric elements:
   - *Broad jump*: One to four bottles lying on their side to jump over
   - *Spatial awareness*: Bottles standing up to weave in and out of

2. To keep interest high, add an additional bottle after each person has had one turn. I like to say something like, "You were so good at jumping over two bottles, do you think you could jump over three and weave through four?" I find children get excited about the challenge and are happy to prove to me that they can!

3. When appropriate, ask children to vary their movements by jumping sideways or backward. This is a little harder to do, but even the trying to do it is a good motor control experience.

4. Incorporating the elements of high jumping, broad jumping, and weaving, place the obstacles in a circle. Widen the circle by adding other elements, such as a balance beam or rocker board. By forming a large circle, all the children can do the course at the same time. No more waiting for their turn! I like to do this version after everyone has had two turns each. I figure they have done enough patient waiting and get to just go!

5. Allow one or more children at a time to set up the obstacle course in a configuration of their own choosing.

VIDEO

http://gameslady.com/video/bottlegames/5-Bottles-obstacle1.asp

Rope Games

A rope, the longer the better, can be used to promote many gross motor skills. A rope is likely to be in your house to use with your children; or if you are a traveling therapist, it's easy to tuck in your bag and take with you.

You can get so many activities from this single piece of equipment. This series of games involves running, jumping, and leaping, so it is easy to get the siblings involved at home or the classmates at school. If you don't have a rope, no worries, you can use scarves, ribbons, or even tube socks tied together.

Setup for Rope Games 1 Through 9

Ideally, you have three adults to work each of these games if you are in a classroom. Two hold the ends of the rope, and one directs traffic. If there aren't two people to hold the ends of a rope, tie one end to a table leg, and that will work fine. You could also choose one of the children to hold the rope or have them take turns holding the rope. A child in a wheelchair, for example, could be an important and needed participant in this way.

Traffic needs to be controlled to keep the flow of traffic going in the same direction and to avoid head-on collisions or traffic jams. Sometimes a child wants to double back and run into the next child taking his turn. So make it clear before beginning that after each turn, the child goes to the end of the line. You may want to have a child demonstrate jumping over the rope and then going back to the line.

What Is Being Learned

The following skills are being reinforced in these games.

SENSORY SKILLS

Vestibular feedback: Running, jumping, hopping, and leaping all involve the vestibular system, as balance is being challenged. You'll see some children jump over the rope and "pretend" to fall on the other side. These children may be doing "their own thing," but just as likely this is a camouflage move to help disguise the fact that their balance is shaky. You can either ignore this in an effort not to encourage a camouflage move with attention or ask the children to do the activity in slow motion. This will give more time to accomplish the skill.

Proprioceptive feedback: Recognizing how much energy it takes to jump over an increasingly higher rope encourages body awareness. Feeling the difference between jumping over a rope and leaping over a rope also stimulates an awareness of how to move one's body in different ways.

Spatial awareness: When children have to keep lowering their body to go under a rope that gets increasingly lower, they need to be aware of how much space their body takes up. Watch for the child who belly crawls to go under a rope when a simple crouch would do, or the child whose back or head keeps hitting the rope because he doesn't crouch down enough. These children might need separate activities to encourage more awareness of body space (such as crawling through tunnels, completing obstacle courses with things to go under, and so on).

SOCIAL SKILLS

Awareness of others: These games move quickly, so there is not much waiting. Still, there is an awareness of others because, as explained earlier, children cannot retrace their steps and bang into their peers.

Game 1: Rising Rope

SETUP

The rope, held between two seated adults, is first placed directly on the floor. Everyone gets a turn to jump over it, landing on two feet. In the next round, the rope is raised higher. Continue in this manner, stopping before the rope is too high to safely go over.

DIRECTIONS

Ask the children to jump over the rope. After they have all had a turn, explain that you are going to make the rope higher and have everyone jump again. After complimenting all the children on their ability to jump over the higher rope, ask, "Should I make it higher?" If my considerable experience is any guide, the children will enthusiastically say, "Yes!" Each time before you raise the rope, ask the question again. I find it fun to act incredulous that they could want to make it higher. "Are you sure?" I might say, "That's pretty high." When it looks like the kids are starting to struggle with the height, move on to the next game.

How high is too high depends on the skill levels of the children in your group. About ten inches is typical. If a child looks like she might be about to trip, the adults should lower or drop the rope and hold the child's hand, if necessary.

VIDEO

http://gameslady.com/video/ropevid/1-raising-up.asp

Game 2: Lowering Rope

SETUP

In the next phase, the rope begins high for children to go under and then gets progressively lower.

DIRECTIONS

Start the rope at a height that requires children to bend their head to go under it. You will keep lowering the rope on each round until the children need to do a belly crawl to go under it without touching. For added fun, tell the children that the rope is sizzling hot. Touch it and make a sizzle sound, and pull your hand away quickly as if the rope is too hot to touch. Ask them, for their own "protection," not to touch the rope with any part of their body as they go under. Even while they are going under, one by one, admonish them to "Be Careful!" (If you have a child with very concrete thinking, you might need to remind the group that this is just pretend and that the rope is not really hot. And you can let that child touch the rope to be sure.)

VIDEO

http://gameslady.com/video/ropevid/2-lowering.asp

Game 3: Over and Under

SETUP

You need at least two ropes in this game. Or, if you have a long rope, you can double (and triple) it. The ropes are held parallel to each other with about a foot between each rope.

One length of rope is held higher than the other. There are two variables: one is how low and how high the ropes are held; the other is which movement comes first, the jumping over or the going under.

DIRECTIONS

Have the children go under the higher rope and jump over the lower. After everyone has had one or two turns with one configuration, change it. Make the other rope low and the other one higher.

VARIATION

A third rope can create more possibilities! With three ropes, the children follow such patterns as over-under-over, under-over-under, or over-over-under. The changes they must make in their body to go, for example, from stooping to standing and jumping require motor control.

VIDEO

http://gameslady.com/video/ropevid/3a-over-under.asp

Game 4: Jump Twice—Forward, Sideways, and Backward

SETUP

As in the previous game, the two ropes are beside each other. Have between five and eight inches between the ropes. Start by having the ropes lying directly on the ground. Raise them slightly when you feel children are ready for a bigger challenge.

DIRECTIONS

The children are to jump twice in a row by going over both ropes. It helps to repeat the words "jump, jump" to give them a rhythm. Start by having them jump forward, a way with which they are already familiar. Then, have them jump sideways twice. The first time they lead with the right side of their body. The second time they lead with the left side. After jumping forward and sideways over both ropes, have them jump backward twice.

VIDEO

http://gameslady.com/video/ropevid/4-bkwrds-sideways.asp

Game 5: Hop Once, Hop Twice

SETUP

In the first phase, use one rope. In the second phase, in which the child hops twice, use two ropes with a space of about a foot or more between them.

DIRECTIONS

First, the child hops on one foot once over one rope. The second time, the two ropes are spread apart and the child hops twice.

For children who are less experienced or less coordinated, you might need to explicitly show how to lift one leg and then hop on the other leg. The lifted leg stays bent the whole time. New hoppers tend to want to land on the foot that was lifted. Sometimes it's helpful for the child to hold the bent leg with his hand to help him remember not to use it for landing. After the first few hops, switch legs.

VIDEO

http://gameslady.com/video/ropevid/5-hop.asp

Game 6: Jump the Creek

SETUP

Lay out two parallel ropes that are about six inches apart. As the game progresses and the "creek" gets wider, make the distance between the two ropes wider.

DIRECTIONS

If you want, have children picture the image of a creek or brook that they must jump over. In the image, more rain falls and the creek gets wider and a little more difficult to jump over. Keep widening the space between the ropes as you tell the story. Do it a small amount, say six inches, each time—until the creek gets almost too wide to jump over.

Depending on the length of the rope, three or more children can jump at the same time. You can signal the jump with a cue, such as "One, two, three—jump!" or "Ready, set, GO."

VIDEO

http://gameslady.com/video/ropevid/6-leap-wide-creek.asp

Game 7: Run and Leap

SETUP

Set up a mat about six or more feet from the rope. The mat indicates where the child is to stand before she begins to run and leap over the rope. Hold the rope above the ground. How high depends on the skill levels of your children. The height can be changed each time, but be prepared to drop or lower the rope if it appears that the child is not leaping high enough to clear the rope and might trip.

DIRECTIONS

Children start from the mat, and then run as fast as they can to the rope and leap over it with one leg leading. They are experiencing the difference between leaping with one leg leading and jumping with and landing on two feet. To get the feel and fun of leaping, the running start is needed. You can set the rhythm and the timing for the child by doing a drum roll or saying, "Run, run, run, run, run, LEAP!"

VIDEO

http://gameslady.com/video/ropevid/7-run-leap.asp

Game 8: Wiggly Rope

SETUP

Two adults or two responsible older children hold the rope and wiggle it back and forth, keeping it at ground level. For younger or less experienced jumpers, do not raise the rope above ground level in this game because the movement of the rope is enough to concentrate on.

DIRECTIONS

The players are to jump over the wiggly rope without touching it. You can set up the imaginary image of a snake that children need to jump over to avoid touching it. It can be a friendly snake, of course, although some like to turn it into a biting snake to encourage reluctant jumpers to jump quickly.

VIDEO

http://gameslady.com/video/ropevid/8-wavy-snake-.asp

Game 9: Swinging Rope

SETUP

Two adults hold each end of the rope as in a traditional game of jumping rope. Instead of making the rope go around in a circle, however, the adults swing it gently from side to side.

DIRECTIONS

This game is for children who are not yet ready for the traditional game of jumping rope in which the rope goes over their head. In this one, the rope is gently swung from side to side. The children still have to time their jumps to go over the rope when it is swung near them. How slowly or quickly to swing the rope depends on the child. The vigorousness or the gentleness can be modified for each child so everyone is successful. Demonstrate how to jump over the rope at the correct time—when the rope is near, and not when it is swung away. You can give verbal cues, such as "Ready . . . jump!"

VIDEO

http://gameslady.com/video/ropevid/9-swinging.asp

Game 10: Creative Jump

SETUP

Set up one or two ropes. If you use two ropes, have them parallel to each other. How high the ropes are off the ground depends on the skill levels and heights of the children. Because this game is more about being creative than about being motorically challenged, a generic rope height would be below their knees or lower.

DIRECTIONS

Tell the children they can go over the ropes any way they want. They can jump, hop, go sideways, somersault, karate kick, and so on. After a time, ask the children to add a sound to their movements. For instance, they can twirl over the rope while clucking their tongue.

VIDEO

http://gameslady.com/video/ropevid/10-creative.asp

Game 11: Tightrope Walking

SETUP

Lay one rope flat on the floor.

DIRECTIONS

Have the children walk on top of the rope as if it were a tightrope in the air. Tell them, "Don't fall off!"

Game 12: Tug-of-War

SETUP

Divide the class into two teams. One team is holding on to one end of the rope. The other team holds on to the other end.

DIRECTIONS

This final game is sure to use the last of their energy. Both teams pull on their end of the rope and try to drag the other children toward them. This can be a goalless game, with both teams pulling and having fun using all their strength. Alternately, draw a line on the floor in the center, and the team that pulls the other group over the line wins.

Rocker Board Games

A rocker board or balance board can be purchased or made. It is basically a piece of plywood with rockers or a cube underneath that makes it rock

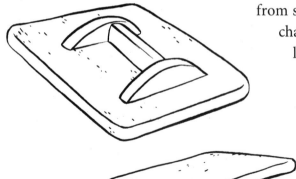

from side to side. The point of a these boards is to challenge one's balance and stimulate the vestibular system.

There are many boards that are designed for one person to use, but if you want to work on social skills as well as balance, use one that is larger so two or more small children can stand on it at the same time. Then, let the fun begin!

What Is Being Learned

The following skills are being reinforced in these games.

SENSORY SKILLS

Vestibular feedback: Rocking on the board encourages children to be aware of how they need to stand to stay upright. To jump off a moving board, children need to be able to find their center of balance and jump from there to land on their feet.

Proprioceptive feedback: Knowing how to move to make the board rock in two different directions—side to side and back and forth—requires awareness of how to control the hip and knee muscles.

MOTOR SKILLS

Children learn to be aware of the subtleties of the movements needed. For example, a deeper knee bend will result in a more exciting rocking movement, and continual adjustment of the depth of that bend will result in better balance. In one game the child is sitting rather than standing on the moving rocker board with legs crisscrossed. This position on a moving surface works on upper trunk and core control to maintain balance.

SOCIAL SKILLS

Awareness of others: This series of games begins with an individual activity. Each child gets the experience of seeing how to move and how to keep balanced. Next, other children are added to increase the balance challenge and to make the kids aware of how to adjust their movements to stay in sync with each other.

Rhythm and timing: There are songs sung to establish a rhythm. These songs or chants can be sped up or slowed down to accommodate different skill levels or to increase the challenge.

Taking turns: Children may be excited for their turn to happen and want to jump up saying, "Me! What about me!?" Singing along while watching others helps them be active and learn patience.

Creativity: At the end of this series, children are given the chance to make up their own versions of how to use the equipment. Because others are involved in the creative process, they get experience in cooperation and consensus.

Setup for All the Rocker Board Games

Make sure there is plenty of room around the rocker board so kids have the space to jump off. You can help minimize children's risk of falling while jumping off by spotting them and adjusting their balance as needed. In one game the child is purposely slid off the board while sitting to give her the experience of falling and recovering. Put a mat or marker on the floor behind the rocker board to show where to stand before stepping onto the board.

Game 1: Rock and Roll

DIRECTIONS

One at a time, each child stands on the board, facing forward, and given as much assistance as needed or wanted. The child's feet are parallel to each other. Hold a child's hand, hold both hands, or hold his hips on the first run-through. Fade the assist as his sense of balance increases. Children let you know with words or a flick of their body when they want to go it alone.

Sing a song to establish a rhythm as well as give them instructions on what to do: this song is sung to the tune of "Skip to My Lou." If you don't know this tune, feel free to make up your own song and tune to establish a specific rhythm:

> Rock and rock and rock and roll
>
> Rock and rock and rock and roll
>
> Rock and rock and rock and roll
>
> Rock and roll and jump off

As each child stands on the board, direct him or her to alternately bend each leg to make the rocker board rock. Then have all the children sing the song just given, with the child on the board jumping off when the "and jump off" words are sung.

VIDEO

http://gameslady.com/video/rockerboard/1-r-side-to-side-copy.asp

Game 2: Back and Forth

DIRECTIONS

Have the child stand on the board facing sideways, with one foot placed comfortably behind the heel of the other. In the previous game, the player faces forward with feet parallel and makes the board rock from side to side. In this game, the player has turned her body 180 degrees and is making the board rock forward and backward. Instead of having her go from one side of her body to the other, ask the child to continually switch her weight from her front leg to the back to make the board rock forward and backward.

VIDEO

http://gameslady.com/video/rockerboard/2-r-back-and-forth.asp

Game 3: Two Together

DIRECTIONS

Place one child behind another to rock together. In this game, both children are facing forward and will make the board rock from one side to the other. Have the first child establish his balance before the next child steps onto the board. Or, hold the board steady until both children are comfortably on. Be sure that the children are holding on to each other, either by arms around a waist or by hands on shoulders. This touching increases the awareness of working with the movements of another. Children can also be standing next to each other instead of one behind the other. Begin to sing the song from Game 1, and if there are others, have them all sing together. Have the children rock together. When it comes time to jump off, repeat the "and jump off" line twice so that each has a turn to jump separately.

VIDEO

http://gameslady.com/video/rockerboard/3a-r-two-together.asp

Game 4: Balance and Slide Off

DIRECTIONS

Have the child sit cross-legged on the board rather than stand and place both hands on knees. How vigorously or how gently you rock the board depends on the skill level of the child and the level of challenge you want to establish. The amount of rocking can also be slowly increased, as the child gets more secure with the rhythm and her sense of balance.

Sing this song (to the tune of "Alouette") as you rock each child. Once the children learn it, have everyone sing it too.

> Can you keep your balance?
> Your balance, your balance
> Can you keep your balance?
> Or will you fall off?!

The surprise ending is that the board gets tilted on the words "Or will you fall off?" so that the child slides off. It's always a surprise for the first child. Usually she isn't sure it was done on purpose. By the second child's turn, all the children know, and then they all get excited for their turn.

Vary the direction of the tilt from one side to another. Even though the board only tilts from side to side, you can lift it up and have the children slide off forward or backward as well. (I sometimes elicit help with the lifting from the other kids.) You can also add a pause before saying the last line or vary the speed with which you say the last line. This adds the fun of the unexpected to the game. They know they are going to fall off but don't know in which direction and don't know when.

VIDEO

http://gameslady.com/video/rockerboard/4-r-balance-and-slide-off.asp

Game 5: Group Rock

DIRECTIONS

Allow more than one child on the board, and allow two or more children to rock the board. How many children can stand on the board and how many can rock will depend on children's awareness of others. Too many children, too vigorous a rock, might mean the game can't even last until the end of the song. The children can establish the direction, and you and any other adults can spot the children and make sure that the game doesn't get out of control so that everyone is safe.

VIDEO

http://gameslady.com/video/rockerboard/5-r-group-rock.asp

Game 6: All New Ways

DIRECTIONS

Once children have had many turns and feel fairly secure and comfortable with the equipment, let them have time to experiment with their own innovative ways to use the rocker board. I find children can be amazingly creative in coming up with new ways to accommodate and include many children and even the teacher in the game. This freedom to invent provides opportunities for creativity in helping each other make the games work. Check out the video to see some of the variations our children came up with. As in the previous game, our job is to allow creativity but to keep it safe.

VIDEO

http://gameslady.com/video/rockerboard/6-new-ways.asp

Don't Rush Arnold

Arnold is a child with Down syndrome. He's three years old but very small for his age, and he has those loose joints that are often seen in children with Down syndrome. As a former dancer, I can't help but envy Arnold's ability to do the splits. Arnold has another skill that Gandhi would admire: he is the master of passive resistance. Gandhi, Martin Luther King Jr., and other proponents of peace would advise protesters not to fight but instead to show their resistance by going limp. A limp body is difficult to move.

Every day Arnold's mom would bring him to the Head Start center for school, and every day he would be invited to join his classmates in morning circle. His response would be to go to another part of the room, turn his back to the circle, and play quietly with a toy. Morning circle is usually not optional at this Head Start center, so several times the teacher would attempt to pick Arnold up and carry him to the circle. That's when we found out that Arnold could turn his body into liquid and slither away. He'd return to his spot, his back to the group.

Arnold had the same passive resistance response to games. Trying to guide him across the balance beam in an obstacle course activity or to get him to jump from square to square was like trying to get mercury to hold its shape. Everybody was having fun, but Arnold would not join in.

We gave up. But slowly Arnold's behavior began to change. He stopped turning his back and began watching the group from a distance. Little by little he got closer, until one day he actually joined the group for good. We were singing "Itsy Bitsy Spider," and Arnold watched everyone as if they were friendly aliens. It didn't occur to him, yet, that he, too, could imitate what others were doing. But we were all over the moon that Arnold actually sat in the circle! We took a video that morning, and when we later showed it at a workshop, someone commented that Arnold wasn't joining in. We said, "You have no idea. That was Arnold really joining in."

As the year progressed, Arnold got braver and braver and eventually joined all the activities, laughing and smiling and being part of the group. At the school year's end, the "graduating" class went over to visit the kindergarten program at the elementary school next door. We wondered how Arnold would do in the new setting. We walked into the classroom, and the children were all sitting on the carpet in a circle. Arnold was the first to walk right over and sit down as if he'd been comfortable doing it all his life.

Arnold taught me an important lesson: all children have their own pace and their own timing. My job is to honor their choices and trust the process.

Therapy Games for Ages Three to Twelve

Karen Beardsley

The therapy games that follow are grouped into skill categories, some of which can be played with only one child, and some of which can have up to a dozen children. I have included the section Social Skills Games, as this book is inherently about inclusion. With children on the autism spectrum in particular, social integration is the area that many parents seem to struggle with the most. We ultimately all would like our children to have friends, to be happy, and just to be able to play with others.

I have selected various games that children and I like to play, and recommended simple materials that I have available to me. For example, if you notice a child is struggling with hand coordination—for example, she does not have adequate control to properly grasp a pencil to draw, or hold a spoon to scoop her food, or even use her fingertips to pull her socks on—you might want to look at the "Rainbow Pizza" game in Fine Motor Games. This game specifically requires the child to develop the small pinching muscles of the hand and fingers, which are necessary for writing and eating and dressing skills. It also reinforces teaching children colors. Likewise, if your child has a hard time playing with others or is not interested in making eye contact or even looking at adults or other children around him, you might choose the game

"The Magician" in the Social Skills Games. Here he will have a fun opportunity to specifically practice sustaining joint attention by having to look at and pay very close attention to another individual, as well as practice turn taking and winning and losing. These are all essential social and emotional building blocks for children in developing relationships and learning to play cooperatively with others. All these therapy games have been selected not only with the development of specific skills in mind but ultimately, and most important, to support children's confidence and self-esteem as they develop and grow.

This book's appendix provides some notes about therapy in the home, including how home-based services might differ from services provided in a clinical or school setting, the benefits of using these simple games at home, as well as some tips for maximizing your sessions for all involved.

Fine Motor Games

Game 1: Ping-Pong Pool

GOALS

Hand grip strength
Eye-hand coordination
Visual tracking skills
Turn taking
Counting
Gross motor skills (if crawling along the floor)

MATERIALS

One turkey baster or nasal aspirator per person, two or three Ping-Pong balls, masking tape or chalk, and two or more players

SETUP

Children can play this game on a table surface or lying flat on a smooth floor. Draw or mark borders for two one-foot-wide goal posts, one at each end of the playing area, with chalk or tape. The two players face each other, with one behind each goal. Give each player a turkey baster (or nasal aspirator) and place two or three Ping-Pong balls in the middle of the playing area.

DIRECTIONS

On a count of three, both players squeeze the turkey basters to blow air at the Ping-Pong balls. Players may not touch the balls, moving them only by air bursts. The players should keep squeezing until all of the balls go past one of the goal posts. Keep score of how many goals each player gets.

MODIFICATIONS

1. Players can race parallel to each other and see who can move his or her ball across the floor the fastest.

2. Players can take turns and count five squeezes each. Keep switching until the ball goes over the goal line.

3. Two or more players can work together taking turns blowing at one Ping-Pong ball until it crosses the goal line. Count how many squeezes it takes total.

Game 2: Punch'n Poke

GOALS

Upper extremity coordination
Eye-hand coordination
Tripod grasp
Visual perceptual skills

MATERIALS

Computer printer paper (can be cut in half), a piece of carpet or panel from a cardboard box big enough to place under the paper, markers, a fine-tip ballpoint pen or sharpened pencil, tape, and one or more players

SETUP

Using a marker, trace or draw a simple outline of a picture (for example, tracing around an object like a cup or creating a simple line drawing of an animal or car or letter in your child's name). Place the paper on a piece of carpet or cardboard with the drawing facing up. Tape the paper down as necessary.

DIRECTIONS

The child punches or pokes the tip of the pen (or pencil) through the paper to make small holes, following the outline of the drawing. Hold the paper up to a light or the window afterward to see the light shine through.

MODIFICATIONS

1. Angle the carpet or cardboard by securing it to an easel or taping it to the wall for better positioning to engage the child's shoulder and full arm.

2. The child can draw a maze or racetrack for another player to try to follow.

3. Some children may have a hard time with their tripod grasp. You can build up the tip of the pen's handle and wrap it with tape or a wad of clay to facilitate a more functional grasp.

Game 3: Rainbow Pizza

GOALS

Bilateral motor coordination
Pinch strength
Matching skills
Turn taking

MATERIALS

One large white paper plate per person; eight colored markers, crayons, or colored pencils; eight clothespins per plate; eight small pieces of paper (squares with one-inch sides); and two or more players

SETUP

Draw four lines evenly intersecting each paper plate so there are eight triangles (like cutting a pizza). Color a small circle or dot on each of the eight small pieces of paper such that all eight different colors are represented. Have players color each triangle in a different color on their individual plates. Put all eight small pieces of colored paper facedown in the middle.

DIRECTIONS

Each person takes turns flipping over one small piece of paper to see what color it is. The person who flips the paper then clips a clothespin onto the edge of that colored "slice" on his plate and returns the colored paper to the center facedown. Then the next player goes. If a player picks a color he already picked, he returns it to the pile, and the next player goes. When a player has a clothespin clipped on each colored slice, he yells, "Rainbow pizza!"

MODIFICATIONS

1. For younger children you can simplify the pizza with fewer colors, or you can put colored dots on the clothespins themselves and match the clothespins to the pizza slices.

2. Some children may lack dexterity and strength and try to use a lateral pinch, whereby they press their thumb pad on the side of their index finger, but ultimately you want to encourage the use of a pincer grasp, whereby the tip of their thumb touches their fingertip.

3. You can also increase the challenge by having children switch the hand they use to clip the clothespins.

Game 4: Snip Snip Clip

GOALS

Prehensile grasp
Fine motor strength
Bilateral motor coordination
Counting
Perceptual motor skills for tracing, coloring, and cutting
Self-help skills

MATERIALS

Two paper plates per child, colored markers or pencils, scissors, and small nail clippers

SETUP

Help the child or children with tracing each hand onto the flat surface of a paper plate, and then cut the hand tracings out.

DIRECTIONS

Show the child how to draw colored fingernails on each tip of the ten fingers. The child can color all nails the same color or each one a different color. When finished, have the child use the nail clipper to snip the fingernails.

VARIATION

Use this game to teach colors by coloring each nail a different color, then hiding the ten markers (or pencils) in a bag. The child reaches in to select a colored marker, and then cuts the matching nail. Or you specify the color, and the child has to find it in the bag.

MODIFICATIONS

1. You will have to experiment with the type of paper plate, as some will work better than others. Some types of firm paper can also work.

2. The child may need you to stabilize her hand if she cannot both hold the paper and clip the nails.

3. If a child cannot manage a small nail clipper, you can also try a small pair of curved nail scissors.

Game 5: Flipping Pancakes

GOALS

Fine motor forearm coordination: supination and pronation
Motor planning skills: speed and dexterity
Bilateral hand coordination
Perceptual motor skills
Counting
Left-to-right sequencing

MATERIALS

One spatula per player; a deck of cards; a bed or soft couch; a timer
(it can be a wind-up timer, wristwatch, lava bubble timer, or sand
timer); and two or more players

SETUP

This game is more fun with two people playing simultaneously, but players
can also take turns. Each of the players will stand (or kneel) on opposite
sides of the bed and lay the entire deck of cards on the bed, either faceup or
facedown (they all have to be the same way when you start).

DIRECTIONS

Tell the child you are going to see who can flip the most "pancakes" in one
minute. When you say "Ready, set, flip," you start the timer, and the child
uses the spatula to turn over to the opposite side as many cards as she can.
When one minute is up you say, "Time's up" or "It's pancake time!" and
count the number of pancakes flipped.

Watch that children don't move their feet and body too much, and
encourage them to use their arms.

MODIFICATIONS

1. If one minute is too long, make it less.

2. It may be difficult for some children to control the spatula. You can
   also try tongs and make the pancakes "hamburgers." Small tongs are
   better for using one hand, which is the ultimate goal in this game.

3. Increase the challenge by having them flip with both their left and
   their right hand, or even have them use two spatulas and flip with both
   hands simultaneously.

4. You can also have them line up the cards and flip starting from left to
   right. They will become "Master Pancake Flippers!"

Game 6: The Rain House

GOALS

Fine motor coordination
Eye-hand coordination
Fine pincer grasp
Bilateral motor coordination
Perceptual motor skills

MATERIALS

A table large enough for children to sit under; pieces of newspaper
(or any large pieces of paper—shiny paper, crepe paper, old
gift wrapping paper), masking tape; scissors; and a marker
(optional)

SETUP

Tape the paper all around the edges of the table so it hangs down in sheets.

DIRECTIONS

Have the child sit or kneel on the floor, either under or next to the
table. Have the child use scissors to cut long strips in the paper, starting
from the bottom of the paper and going right up to the top edge. The child
continues cutting until all the paper is cut in strips, and then you and the
child can sit under the table and watch the rain falling down!

MODIFICATIONS

1. For some children who are struggling with learning cutting skills,
   this is a nice activity: it naturally positions the forearm and hand in a
   thumbs-up position, which makes cutting with scissors easier.

2. You can also draw vertical lines that give visual guidelines for a child to cut along.

3. If a child really struggles with the scissors, have him use his hands to rip strips upward in the paper.

Game 7: Tongs and Tweezers

GOALS

Fine motor coordination

Fine pincer grasp

Bilateral motor coordination

Counting

MATERIALS

One pair of large kitchen tongs or one pair of tweezers; an empty egg carton; an empty water bottle or jar; and colored pom-pom balls or small rolled-up balls of colored paper, balls of clay, or even cotton balls

SETUP

Place all balls into a jar and clear a place on the floor on which the child can comfortably work. (Alternately, a table could be used as a work surface.)

DIRECTIONS

Shake the balls up in the jar and dump them out on the floor. Have the child use the tongs or tweezers she selected to try to pick them up, one by one, and put each ball into an empty egg carton slot or back into the jar. Have the child count the balls one by one as they are placed, or count along with her if needed.

MODIFICATIONS

1. Some children may need to start by using two hands to manipulate the tongs or tweezers.

2. You can add challenge by setting a timer to see how fast the child can pick up all the balls. You could also have the child try alternating hands.

3. You can also make tongs by wedging a small rubber eraser between two chopsticks, about a third of the way from one end, and then tightly wrapping a rubber band around the chopsticks at that end so the eraser is held snugly in between.

Game 8: A, B, . . . Can You C Me?

GOALS

Fine manipulative pincer grasp
Handwriting
Visual perceptual skills
Left-to-right sequencing
Tactile processing

MATERIALS

A plain piece of paper (at least the size of computer printer paper) or posterboard or cardboard, plus a separate piece of blank paper; markers; a ruler; ten pennies or any similar small coins (all the same); and a pencil

SETUP

Prepare the piece of paper or posterboard by drawing grid lines (seven vertical and seven horizontal) so you have forty-nine small boxed squares. Write all the alphabet letters scattered randomly in the boxes (some letters will be used twice).

DIRECTIONS

Decide in advance what word the child will try to spell. Call out the first letter from that word and have the child place a coin on that letter space on the grid and write the letter down. Have the child write the letters, if able, on a separate piece of paper. Continue until the whole word is spelled out on paper.

MODIFICATIONS

1. Depending on the skill level of child, you can add as many grids and letters as needed. The words can be as simple as "CAT" or as complicated as "EXCELLENT"!

2. You can simplify the game by writing the letter on a piece of paper and asking the child to match it, or you can make it more challenging by sounding the letter out phonetically or even drawing it on the child's back or on the palm of his hand with his eyes closed.

3. If working with a very early speller, you can make six vertical and five horizontal lines, for a total of thirty boxes.

Game 9: Pumpkin Head

GOALS

Eye-hand coordination
Visual perceptual skills
Fine motor strength
Design copying
Eye tracking
Tactile stimulation

MATERIALS

A large pumpkin or gourd or a block of Styrofoam (even a cardboard box can work), a thick marker, a small wooden or plastic children's hammer or wood mallet, at least fifteen to twenty golf tees, and a flashlight

SETUP

Have the child draw a face on the side of the pumpkin (or Styrofoam block or box) using the marker. You can assist her in drawing it. If you are using a pumpkin, have the child help you scoop the insides out.

DIRECTIONS

Have the child hammer the golf tees following the line drawing of the face. If you have enough tees, you can leave them in, or you can have the child help you pull them out only leaving the holes. At the end, have the child put a flashlight into the pumpkin to shine through the holes.

MODIFICATIONS

1. Some children may not be able to follow the lines. You can simplify the drawing or just allow them to hammer away anywhere, as most younger children like to do.

2. You can write letters or numbers instead of a drawing, or have children draw their own designs as well.

3. If a long-handled hammer is too difficult to manipulate, the child can also try banging in the tees with a tennis ball or even a rock.

4. Some children may not like the texture of pumpkin goop on their hands, so give them a large spoon to scoop.

Game 10: Penny Race

GOALS

Fine motor manipulation and dexterity
Tactile processing in hands
Bilateral motor coordination
Left-to-right sequencing
Visual perceptual sequencing

MATERIALS

A piece of paper (twelve by four inches), a pencil, and ten pennies (or any small coins)

SETUP

Helping as necessary, have the child trace around a penny so that you have ten consecutive circles in a row, each about one inch apart across the twelve-inch piece of paper.

DIRECTIONS

Have the child start with five coins in one hand. When you say "go," he will have to place each coin on each circle as fast as he can using only that hand, working left to right. If more than one coin drops out, he has to start again. Count how many seconds it takes. Then see if he can work up to ten coins. Next have him switch to the opposite hand to do the same. Then have the child divide the coins between both hands so he has five in each and try to place them simultaneously from both hands. Ask the child to try to beat his own record!

MODIFICATIONS

1. You can also use kidney beans, small marbles, or pebbles. The size of the items will depend on how many a child can realistically manipulate in his hand. Some children might only be able to start with three items.

2. Using two hands together might be too difficult for some children, in which case you can say, "Left, then right, then left, then right," and so on.

Gross Motor Games

Game 1: Flying Meteorite

GOALS

Bilateral upper extremity coordination
Crossing midline
Perceptual motor skills: eye tracking and depth perception
Balance and equilibrium

MATERIALS

A Frisbee; a ball; a piece of string long enough to hang the ball suspended from a fixed point, such as a tree branch or crossbeam; and two players

SETUP

Securely tie one end of the string around the ball. You will need a place to tie the other end, such as a tree limb, a beam in a carport, or a swing set bar, so that the ball can hang and freely swing at about the height of the child's chest.

DIRECTIONS

Swing the ball gently by pushing it in different directions. The child holds the Frisbee with two hands so that the flat end will make contact with the ball to push it away. The idea is to protect the earth from the meteorite by propelling it away again and again and not to let the "meteorite" hit any part of his body as well. This takes constant moving, dodging, turning, and hitting the ball. After one minute, switch turns and count how many times each person "hits the meteorite and saves the earth"!

MODIFICATIONS

1. You can substitute a firm plastic plate or other flat hard object for the Frisbee. You could also use a paddleball or tennis racket, but encourage the use of two hands. The key is that the item has to be big enough to hold with two hands.

2. You can vary the challenge by using a larger or smaller ball depending on the child's skill level. A beach ball is lighter and moves more slowly, whereas a tennis ball increases the challenge.

Game 2: Circus Hoop

GOALS

Perceptual motor skills
Eye tracking
Gross motor coordination
Motor planning
Grasping and releasing
Counting

MATERIALS

A Hula-Hoop, five balls or five beanbags, chalk or tape, and two or more players

SETUP

Mark a space on the floor from which players will throw the balls (or bean-bags). The adult holds the Hula-Hoop sideways starting low down on the ground some distance from the mark on the floor. The child stands on the marked spot on the floor to throw the balls.

DIRECTIONS

The child tries to throw a ball through the hoop. The player with the hoop moves it up one foot at a time after each turn until all five balls have been thrown.

Have the child count as each one is thrown.

MODIFICATIONS

1. The child's position can be moved closer or further away depending on skill level.

2. You can use large balls (nine-inch balls or beach balls) that require the use of two hands or small balls to work on a one-handed throw.

Game 3: Fire Twirler!

GOALS

Bilateral coordination
Left-right discrimination
Motor planning
Directionality
Following directions

MATERIALS

For each child: one pair of chopsticks, two 1.5-foot pieces of string, a sheet of newspaper, masking tape, and a red streamer or ribbon (optional); and one to two children

SETUP

For each player, crumple the newspaper into two balls, and, if you want, tape or tie a red streamer to each. Tie the string around each paper ball, and tie the other end of the string to the two chopstick ends so that the ball hangs no more than one foot from each chopstick.

DIRECTIONS

Have each child stand with feet shoulder distance apart, holding the end of one chopstick in each hand. Have them first extend their right arm and gently swirl their right hand, with the ball hanging toward the floor like a pendulum, moving clockwise. Then have them put their right hand down and extend their left arm straight out, swirling the ball in a counterclockwise motion. Next have them put both hands out together and swirl the balls in opposite directions.

MODIFICATIONS

1. Depending on their skill level, you can have children experiment with using one hand or two hands together. You can call out different directions, like "Right arm out, left arm in, twirl both to the right, twirl both to the left."

2. You can add walking, standing on one foot, balancing on a rocker board, playing with eyes closed, and so on to make it more challenging.

Game 4: Choo-Choo Train

GOALS

Proprioceptive "heavy work"
Bilateral motor coordination

Perceptual motor skills

Gross motor skills

MATERIALS

A laundry basket, a jump rope or piece of strong string, books, stuffed animals, and dolls

SETUP

Find a space large enough to walk around pulling the basket (one with floors that won't get scratched). Tie both ends of the jump rope or string to one side of the basket. Layer some heavy books in the bottom of the basket—these can be the seats for the animals and dolls to sit on. Strategically place the animals and dolls in different locations around the house at "train stops."

DIRECTIONS

Have the child stand inside the loop of rope, holding it with both hands so he can walk facing forward pulling the basket behind him. Have him call, "All aboard!" and pull the train to pick up the first passenger (a stuffed toy or doll). After loading the passenger, he should again call, "All aboard!" and proceed to the next stop, until all passengers have boarded the train.

MODIFICATIONS

1. If you have two children, you can tie two ropes and they can pull simultaneously, or they can stand one behind the other tugging a single rope.
2. You could have the child walk backward.
3. You can vary the weight of the items in the basket according to the child's strength, and he can even pull a friend!

Game 5: Don't Forget the Shoes!

GOALS

Teamwork
Bilateral and fine motor coordination
Gross motor skills
Sequencing
Following directions
Tactile stimulation

MATERIALS

Per team (of at least four to six children): one set of larger-size clothes (for example, shirt, pants, socks, shoes)

SETUP

This is a dressing relay race and is best with a group of at least four or six children, but the more the better. Divide the number of people evenly into two teams (or more, depending on the number of children), and have each team split up, with half standing at one end of the room and the other half standing at the opposite end of the room. Stack a set of clothes in front of the first person on each of the team. These first players should be standing at one end of the room.

DIRECTIONS

When you say "Go!" the first person on each team will dress up in all the clothes as fast as she can, then run across the room to the next in line. She will then take off all the clothes, and that next person will put them all on. Then that person runs back across the room to the next person, and takes the clothes off so the next child can put them all on. Once the last person has dressed completely, he yells, "Done!" and this team is the winner.

MODIFICATIONS

1. Teammates can assist a child with undressing and dressing as needed if she is having a hard time.

2. If a full set of clothes is too much, you can eliminate the socks and shoes or use Velcro straps or elastic-waist pants and pullover shirts (rather than pants with zippers and shirts with buttons). Likewise, to increase the challenge you can add hats, gloves, jackets, lacing, or belts with buckles.

Game 6: Helicopter

GOALS

Gross motor skills: balance and motor planning
Bilateral coordination: jumping, hopping, and skipping
Vestibular input
Perceptual motor eye tracking
Counting

MATERIALS

One three- or four-foot piece of rope or jump rope, chalk, and two or more players

SETUP

Use the chalk to draw a large circle about six feet in diameter, ideally on a sidewalk or driveway or any flat, wide, outdoor space. Ask a child to stand anywhere on the marked circle; this will help her keep her spot. The "Helicopter Flyer," who is likely to be the adult, squats or stands in the middle of the circle holding the rope. If there is more than one child, children can stand anywhere on the marked circle.

DIRECTIONS

When you call, "Countdown: three, two, one, takeoff!" the person in the center starts to swing the rope slowly in circles close to the ground around him, and the child on the circle has to jump over the rope whenever it comes to her feet. Have the jumper count how many times she was able to jump over the rope without touching it or falling. Have players trade places.

MODIFICATIONS

1. The person swinging the rope can modify the speed depending on the skill level of the jumper.

2. The child jumping can initially step over the rope, then jump, hop, or alternate feet. To increase the challenge, the child could also try to jump backward.

3. If you have more than one jumper, they can also walk around on the circle while stepping or jumping over the rope as it passes.

4. You can substitute a long beach towel for the rope.

Game 7: Surf's Up!

GOALS

Vestibular input
Kinesthetic sense
Postural control: balance and equilibrium
Bilateral coordination
Motor planning

MATERIALS

One to three firm cushions; an approximately two-foot-long piece of wood or solid board suitable for standing on, or a small ironing board, kickboard, or boogie board; a plant sprayer bottle filled with water (optional); fun fast music! (optional); and one or more children

SETUP

Stack the cushions on the floor, and place the balancing board centered on top of the pile (like a small seesaw).

DIRECTIONS

Have the child has stand on the board and try to balance his body, rocking back and forth as he "surfs the waves" without falling off. If you want, play the music as the child surfs. You can also squirt water from the sprayer so that the surfer has to try to lean to the side or duck out of the way. If he falls off, you yell, "Wipeout!" Children can take turns surfing and squirting.

MODIFICATIONS

1. Depending on the weight of the child, you can stack several cushions on top of one another. For a heavier child, thicker cushions or a greater number of cushions may need to be stacked. If the tilting is too difficult, you can make it easier by placing a cushion under each end of the board along with the center cushion. If you have a strong board you can also place a firm brick or block of wood under the center instead of a cushion.

2. Make it more of a challenge by having the child switch his feet in the opposite direction, squat down, go on his knees, put his feet close together or further apart, hold his hands out to his sides or on his hips, and so on.

3. For small children, you can try using a large cutting board, large hardcover book, or whiteboard as the balancing board.

Game 8: The Hailstorm

GOALS

Eye-hand coordination
Visual perceptual skills: eye tracking and depth perception
Balance
Bilateral coordination

MATERIALS

An umbrella (or a big plastic bowl or bucket), at least twenty sheets of newspaper, masking tape (optional), an outdoor space, and two to three players

SETUP

Crumple the newspaper into small, tight balls (you can bind them with pieces of tape if you want them to stay wrapped tightly).

DIRECTIONS

One person holds the open umbrella using two hands. Tell her, "The hailstorm is approaching fast." The other players take turns tossing the newspaper balls underhand up high into the sky. The player holding the umbrella has to run under it and line the umbrella up to block the falling "hail" before it hits the ground. All players can gather the hail after all of it has been tossed and keep going as long as they want, or until the person with the umbrella blocks ten hail chunks.

MODIFICATIONS

1. Children can hold the umbrella upside down to try to catch the hail in the umbrella.

2. Instead of using newspaper balls, you can substitute peanuts in shells or other small, light objects to vary the challenge. It is funny for kids to have peanuts rain from the sky.

Game 9: Ready, Aim, Squirt!

GOALS

Hand grip strength
Bilateral coordination
Visual perceptual skills: depth perception
Following directions
Gross motor skills

MATERIALS

Chalk, one plant sprayer bottle per person filled with water,
an outdoor space to draw on the ground, and two players

SETUP

Draw a circle big enough for two to stand in. Then draw two straight lines extending out from it on each side of equal length, each about ten feet long. Two players stand back-to-back in the circle facing outward, with water-filled sprayers in hand.

DIRECTIONS

On the count of three, two children run to the ends of their respective lines, turn, and "fire" their plant sprayer in an attempt to hit the other player within five squirts.

VARIATIONS

1. You can have children do consecutive jumps on two feet to the end of the line before turning and "firing," or you can ask them to hop on one foot or tiptoe.

2. More players can be added to the game. As you keep adding friends, keep adding lines branching out so the circle eventually looks like a sun. The more friends, the wetter you get!

Game 10: Sit, Roll Over, Jump!

GOALS

Gross motor planning
Bilateral coordination
Kinesthetic body awareness
Following directions
Vestibular input

MATERIALS

A large enough space to move about freely, chalk or tape, small token items that can be used as pretend "bones" for treats to feed the "puppies," and three players minimum

SETUP

Use the chalk (or tape) to mark a spot on the ground for each child, spacing the spots at least a full arms' width apart.

DIRECTIONS

All of the children except for one will be the puppies. One child will be the dog trainer. Have all of the puppies move on all fours to take their place on the spot on the floor. The trainer will call out different actions she wants to the puppies to learn (for example, "Sit up, jump, run, sleep, roll over, fetch the ball, play dead"). After each trick, all of the puppies get a treat, and then must return to their spot.

MODIFICATIONS

1. You can demonstrate actions in advance or have the children come up with their own.
2. Add obstacles like pillows to jump over or a table to go under.
3. Puppies can count their treats at the end. You can even use small pretzel nuggets or other edible treats for them to really eat!

Sensory Games

Game 1: Club Sandwich

GOALS

Tactile input
Proprioceptive deep pressure
Sequencing
Counting

MATERIALS

A space large enough to lie comfortably on the floor; blankets, towels, or both of different sizes; sponges; pillows; small cushions; and two to three players

SETUP

Lay all the sandwich "ingredients" around you nearby.

DIRECTIONS

One child starts by lying on her back on a cushion and being the bread on the bottom layer. This child gets to order what ingredients she wants on the sandwich. For example, "butter" (use a sponge to "spread" the butter all over her limbs, hands, feet, shoulders, and stomach); "lettuce" (lay a towel or blanket on top of her); ten tomatoes (hold a washcloth and push ten times all over her body); "cheese" (take a pillow to pat all over her body); and so on. Then put the last piece of "bread" on top (lay another towel, blanket, or cushion). You can add as much or as little as you like. Then, the best part . . . everyone gets to eat the sandwich . . . munch, munch, munch as you scrunch and push firmly but gently down on her body. Have children take turns being the sandwich.

MODIFICATIONS

1. Some children may have tactile defensiveness and may not like light or ticklish types of touching. Firm deep pressure works best. Also be sensitive to the face, neck, and stomach area, and avoid these if the child resists it.

2. You will find you can grab just about any materials to expand on this game.

Game 2: The Mirror

GOALS

Motor planning
Visual perceptual skills
Crossing midline
Understanding directionality and laterality
Bilateral motor coordination

MATERIALS

Two players

SETUP

Have the two players stand facing each other.

DIRECTIONS

One player is the leader, and the other has to copy or "mirror" his exact movements. Some examples might be raising and crossing arms, balancing on one foot, bending to one side, rhythmic repetitive movements, and jumping in place.

MODIFICATIONS

1. Start slowly, but gradually vary the speed and directionality. Up, down, crossing midline, arms and legs together, and also using alternating opposite arm and leg movements.

2. You can even add a ball to bounce, dribble, toss, and catch depending on skill levels.

3. Add facial expressions too!

- -

Game 3: Moon Walker

GOALS

Proprioceptive sensory input
Motor planning
Gross motor coordination
Kinesthetic awareness
Balance

MATERIALS

Ankle or wrist weights or two one-pound bags of beans or rice; a backpack filled with some heavy books; masking tape; four paper plates; basic furniture, such as chairs or foot stools; and an empty box big enough to step into

SETUP

Tape an eight-foot line of masking tape to the floor, and set up a simple obstacle course, which may require lining up a few chairs, placing the four paper plates one foot apart as "moon craters," and setting the box at one end as a landing module so that it becomes a loop. One person wraps the weights around his ankles or tapes the one-pound bag of beans or rice around the top of each shoe. He steps into the landing module. Another child can wear the weighted backpack, or one child can choose to put on ankle weights and the backpack together.

DIRECTIONS

The astronaut wears the "gravity weights" or "moon shoes" or carries the "astronaut oxygen pack" (weighted backpack) on his back. He then proceeds on his journey to walk on the moon, descending from the module (climbing out of the box), climbing large craters (chairs and couches), walking fissures (the tape), jumping over smaller craters (paper plates), and then eventually getting back to the landing module.

MODIFICATIONS

1. A child can take two turns—one with the moon boots and backpack and one without—to see what it feels like with and without gravity.

2. You can vary the journey to go outdoors.

3. Lighten the load or make it heavier based on the size of the child.

Game 4: Lollypop Lick

GOALS

Oral sensory awareness
Tactile stimulation
Taste discrimination
Eye-hand coordination
Oral motor skills
Counting

MATERIALS

A variety of soft-textured dipping foods (that the child can safely taste) like pudding, yogurt, cream cheese, peanut butter, sour cream, salad dressing, salsa, and mustard; one spoon per person; a small tray or easy-wipe placemat; a paper towel and a cup of water per person; and two or more children

SETUP

Place a small dab of each of the textured tastes on the tray or placemat. Be sure you have enough space between each so the tastes don't mix together.

Have the cup of water and paper towel handy for each child to dip and wipe their spoon.

DIRECTIONS

Each person will hold a spoon—this will be the lollypop. You can cue them and say, "Time to dip and lick." Have children take turns dipping the back rounded end of their spoon into a food taste and then licking it off. They then dip their spoon in water and wipe it between tastes. Encourage children to try them all and have them identify which tastes they like and dislike and why. Is it sweet, salty, sour, spicy?

MODIFICATIONS

1. Having the children sit in front of a small mirror so they can watch their mouth and tongue often facilitates this game. It may help divert some of the attention from the difficult task of trying new textures, tastes, and foods.

2. Some children may clearly have an aversion to some of the tastes or textures. Allow them to dip as much or as little as they want. If they don't want to lick a certain taste, they can just dab a tiny amount on the tip of their tongue or even just smell it for starters. Some may even want to mix some of the tastes together.

3. You can also use a real lollypop to dip and lick, as it may provide an incentive for some children to experiment more than they normally would.

4. Expand on the game by having children pair up, with one dipping the lollypop for the other to guess the flavor.

5. Try to present a mix of flavor tastes, such as sweet, salty, sour, and savory.

Game 5: Snowplow

GOALS

Vestibular stimulation
Crossing midline
Bilateral arm coordination
Perceptual motor skills
Gross motor skills

MATERIALS

A space large enough to roll across the floor, cushions or pillows of
various sizes, a big push broom (or any broom), a pillowcase,
string, and at least two players

SETUP

Place the pillowcase over the head of the broom and tie it around the handle
with string (this is to make a barrier over the bristles). Have a child lie flat
on the floor with the pillows (clumps of snow) scattered around her.

DIRECTIONS

The person who is the "snowplow" pushes the broom gently against the person on the floor to help her log-roll across the floor, gathering the cushions
in her path to pile on the side of the room. The snowplow and the person
on the floor may need to change directions to get all the snow cleared off the
floor and piled high on the sides. The players then switch places.

MODIFICATIONS

1. Some children may find it hard to roll while grabbing the cushions.
   They can also just slide them as they move along.
2. Instead of using pillows, you can substitute crumpled pieces of paper
   that children have to grab as they roll by.

Game 6: Natural Disaster

GOALS

Memory recall
Vestibular stimulation
Proprioceptive input
Tactile input
Gross motor planning
Following directions

MATERIALS

A large space on the floor to tumble and move about, and least two
players (the more people, the more fun)

SETUP

First review the game's movements with the children and have them practice. The participants will need to be old enough to follow the directions
and remember multiple items. One person is the designated the "Weather
Announcer."

Earthquake: Kids sit on the floor with their knees grabbed and tucked
up to their chest, then roll and bounce around the room.
Flood: Kids run around the room moving both arms in a freestyle
swimming motion.
Mudslide: Kids lie flat on their stomach and swish their arms and legs
out to both sides (like a frog or as if doing the breaststroke).
Volcano: Kids cross their arms and hold their hands over their ears and
jump up and down.
Hurricane: Kids hold both arms extended straight out to their sides
and twirl quickly around in circles.
Blackout: Kids lie still, flat on their back, with their eyes closed and the
lights out, for one minute.

DIRECTIONS

The Weather Announcer begins by shouting out any one of the preceding natural disasters; the group must recall and follow the movements. "Today we have a hurricane warning . . ."

MODIFICATIONS

1. For some children it may be too difficult to remember all of the directions. Just shorten the list as needed.

2. If there is a large enough group, you can eliminate each child who is the last to perform the movement until there is one survivor.

3. If the group becomes all "revved up" or overstimulated at any given point, or when you are finished, end with a calming down activity and call it a "blackout."

Game 7: Worms and Eyeballs

GOALS

Tactile stimulation
Olfactory stimulation
Bilateral hand coordination
Eye-hand coordination

MATERIALS

One package of cooked spaghetti; one or two tablespoons of oil; water; two spoons per person; a dozen grapes, blueberries, or cherries (or other small round pieces of food or even objects like marbles); a large bowl or serving platter; a timer, watch, or clock; and one to two children minimum

SETUP

Toss the noodles in a little oil and water so they are slimy and don't stick together, and place them in the bowl or on a serving platter. Toss in the grapes or whatever round objects you have to use.

DIRECTIONS

Have kids take turns using a spoon in each hand to fish as many "eyeballs" as they can out of the "worm pit" in one minute.

MODIFICATIONS

1. You can also have kids use a melon baller or tongs in one hand, or even their hands if they are so brave!

2. Add more eyeballs as needed. You can even add a dash of green food coloring to the noodles for special effects.

3. Some children obviously won't like the sensation on their hands, so give these children a long-handled spoon to start with.

Game 8: Bag O Bag

GOALS

Tactile discrimination
Kinesthetic sense
Proprioceptive awareness and motor planning
Memory recall
Fine manipulative skills
Language development and labeling

MATERIALS

A small cloth bag or small pillowcase; at least five or six small common
household items that can fit in the bag, such as a toothbrush, paper
clip, toy car, key, small stuffed animal, comb, pencil, and so on; and
two or more persons

SETUP

Hide all the items in the bag so that no one else sees what they are.

DIRECTIONS

Have each child take a turn. Hold the bag and say, "Bag o bag, shake shake
shake, what will _____ (the child's name) take?" (Children will probably chime
in!) Then the child whose name is called reaches into the bag and feels around
to grab hold of one item, and tries to guess what it is before pulling it out to
look. Continue until, one by one, all the items are removed from the bag.

MODIFICATIONS

1. Make the items relevant to children's developmental age. They should
   be objects with which children are familiar.

2. If children are unable to identify an object by feel, they can pull one
   item out at a time, manipulate it in their hands, and name it before
   putting it back in the bag and trying again.

Game 9: Feed the Otter

GOALS

Tactile stimulation
Core trunk strengthening
Vestibular stimulation
Bilateral eye-hand coordination
Motor planning
Directionality
Counting

MATERIALS

A large enough space on the floor to roll around; big soft blankets or towels; a small pillowcase or a paper or plastic bag; balls, bean-bags, or even crumpled balls of newspaper; and at least three players

SETUP

Lay the blanket (or towels) on the floor (this is the water). Prepare the balls if crumpling newspaper (these are the "fish" to feed the otter).

DIRECTIONS

One person is chosen to be the otter who swims and frolics about. She lies in the middle of the blanket on her back and holds the pillowcase (or bag) open on her belly. The otter "swims" by pushing around on her back or rolling around across the blanket while the feeders try to toss the "fish" (the balls) into the sack on her belly. See how many fish the otter can catch and collect to eat! Each person can take a turn being the otter.

MODIFICATIONS

1. You can scatter pillows on the floor (for rocks) or place a variety of soft, fluffy items (for seaweed) to push around and roll over.

2. A child who doesn't mind having his head covered can also roll up in or "swim" under a blanket or sheet.

3. Some children may even want to attempt somersaults across the floor.

Game 10: Bubble Monster

GOALS

Oral motor skills
Breath control
Lip closure
Tactile stimulation
Eye-hand coordination

MATERIALS

A big bowl (such as a large salad bowl), water, liquid dish soap, one
straw per person, and two to four persons

SETUP

Squirt about one tablespoon of liquid dish soap into the bowl and fill one-
third of the bowl with water.

DIRECTIONS

Have children blow through individual straws placed in the bowl and watch
the bubble monster grow. Kids can all blow together or take turns and see
how big they can make it before it topples over! Many children also like to
pop the bubbles with their fingers.

MODIFICATIONS

1. Some children may confuse blowing with sucking when using a straw,
   so be sure you practice first. Also, some children may not have adequate lip closure to make a complete seal on the straw.
2. You can vary the challenge by using straws of different sizes. Clear
   aquarium tubing works well too, as you can cut it to any length you
   wish. The longer or wider the straw, the more breath control you need.

Social Skills Games

Game 1: Catch the Thief!

GOALS

Developing joint attention

Turn taking

Engaging in pretend play

Learning to react appropriately in a competition

Understanding the rules of an abstract game

MATERIALS

Six household objects (for example: a cup, a book, a toy car, a watch, a pencil, and a coin); masking tape or chalk; and three or more players

SETUP

Make an *X* with masking tape or chalk, and have one person (a designated "thief") stand on that spot. The six items are randomly placed in front of the him, slightly spaced apart (so the thief does not have to rotate his head).

DIRECTIONS

The thief is going to stare at the object he wants to steal, keeping his head very still. The others will pretend they are the police. Each will take turns telling the thief which item he is looking at. Whoever guesses the correct item has stopped the thief from stealing the item, and another person becomes the thief. If someone guesses the wrong item, the thief gets to steal that item and remove it from the pile; he also gets another turn. Keep going until everyone has had a turn or all "treasures" are stolen.

MODIFICATION

You can make it easier or more difficult by using fewer or more items and moving them closer or further away from the thief.

Game 2: What Is It?

GOALS

Turn taking
Cooperation and sharing
Considering a partner's perspective
Problem solving
Fine motor skills
Perceptual motor skills
Group processing

MATERIALS

Blank drawing paper, colored pencils, pens, rulers, cups of different sizes, protractors, any small objects you can trace around, a timer, stencils with various shapes (optional), and two to four players

SETUP

Each person gets a blank piece of paper. All items to be used for tracing are laid out to share, including colored pencils, pens, rulers, protractors, cups, and stencils if you have them. Everyone sits around a table or on the floor to draw.

DIRECTIONS

Set the timer for one minute. Each person begins by making marks or designs on the paper using any of the tools available. When the timer rings, all players pass their paper to the person to the right. The timer is set again for one minute as each person adds to the design on the paper. Keep passing the paper after every minute until everyone has had a round or two, or until you as the facilitator determine that time is up. Each person then holds up the paper and tries to decide and share what it is! Group members can also brainstorm together, as well as share what they intended it to be when it was their turn.

MODIFICATION

If using tools is too challenging, children can just draw by hand with pencils.

Game 3: The Feelings Dance

GOALS

Recognizing and labeling emotions

Visual attention: reading facial expressions of others

Following the rules of a game

Active listening

Participating in a group activity

MATERIALS

A large enough space to move about and dance, paper plates, a marker, a radio or other source of fun dancing music that can be started and stopped, and two or more players

SETUP

Draw an emotion face (for example, sad, happy, angry, surprised, excited, bored, tired . . .) on each paper plate and write the word for that emotion below the face. Lay all the plates facedown around the room so the emotions on them cannot be seen.

DIRECTIONS

Start the music, and have everyone dance around the room. When the music stops, each child jumps onto a paper plate. One at a time, they take turns flipping over the plate they are on. Each child has to make the face of that emotion and name what it is. The music starts again, and the game continues until every player has landed on each plate.

MODIFICATIONS

1. Children can also jump around with two feet, hop on one foot, or skip to land on a plate.

2. To practice developing empathy for others, have a child relate personal experiences to a feeling. You can elaborate by asking each child, "What makes you feel this way?"

3. To practice identifying situations in which one might experience a feeling, ask a child, "When do you feel like this?"

Game 4: Elbow-to-Elbow

GOALS

Tactile and proprioceptive sensory input: physical body awareness of self and partner

Motor planning

Directionality

Gross motor coordination

Fine motor coordination

Perceptual motor skills

Communication

Following directions

Cooperation and considering the partner's perspective

MATERIALS

Simple household items, such as a cup, water, toys, paper, a pencil, a towel, and a ball; and three players minimum

SETUP

Players hook their right elbows so that they are facing in opposite directions.

DIRECTIONS

Give the players simple tasks to do. The team will have to negotiate how to move their bodies through each activity. Some examples of tasks can be:

◆ Go to the laundry and find a towel and fold it.

◆ Pour me a glass of water to drink and bring it here.

◆ Go wash your hands.

◆ Get five toys that you want to play with.

◆ Write your names on this piece of paper.

◆ Play catch with a ball.

MODIFICATIONS

1. If you have more than two children you can keep adding another to the group by hooking elbows, alternating the directions children are facing.

2. For younger children, it is easier to have the pair face the same direction.

3. You can try tying their legs and arms together with a strip of cloth so they have to move as one unit.

4. For older kids, you can have them stand back-to-back and tie them together around their waists so they move as one unit.

Game 5: Stepping Stones

GOALS

Teamwork
Following the rules of a game
Understanding the concept of competition
Motor planning
Sequencing
Communicating with peers

MATERIALS

Enough pillows and cushions of different sizes or pieces of newspaper so that there is always one extra spare pillow or newspaper piece per group of players, and three or more players (ideally an even number, if racing with two teams)

SETUP

Place the pillows (or newspaper pieces folded in half) in a row, one in front of the other, starting at one end of the room. To begin, children each stand on their own pillow, one directly behind the next, starting on the first pillow. The last child in line should have one empty pillow behind her.

DIRECTIONS

Tell the players, "Children, you have to cross the river, and there is a hungry, dangerous crocodile in it. You can't step off the stones or you will be eaten!" The room is the river and the pillows are the stones. While standing on the pillows, the child with the empty pillow behind her must pass it forward to the first person in line. Then the child who is handed the pillow places it down in front of him and steps forward on it. The process keeps repeating until the pair has safely moved across the entire room without being eaten!

MODIFICATIONS

1. If you have several pairs of children, you can make it into a race. Whoever crosses the river first without falling in wins.

2. For teams of more than two, just add one more pillow with every additional child so there is always one extra.

3. You can vary the stepping stones by using chairs, stools, washcloths, or anything children can stand on and climb onto.

Game 6: Pinball

GOALS

Core trunk strengthening
Visual perceptual eye tracking
Eye-hand coordination
Bilateral coordination
Teamwork

MATERIALS

A large playground ball or inflatable beach ball, a large enough floor
space for players to lie on their stomach facing opposite one
another, and at least two players

SETUP

Have two children lie on their stomach facing each other, about five feet
apart. If you have more participants, children can lie in a circle. Each player
has to hook his or her own thumbs together so his or her hands move
together as one unit.

DIRECTIONS

The first player starts by rolling the ball to her partner, pushing with the
palms of both hands. The second player has to push it back fast. If there are
several players, they each push or deflect the ball quickly when it comes to
them. When players hit the ball, they make a funny made-up sound, like
that made by a pinball machine: "ding, dong, boing, ching, bling," and so on.
Count to see how long the children can keep the "pinball" going.

MODIFICATIONS

1. You can have children vary positions, such as sitting with their legs
   open and straight like a *V* and then pushing the ball with both hands,

or sitting and leaning back on their elbows to use the bottoms of both feet to push the ball.

2. If there are many players, each person could pick the sound he or she wants to make, and make only that sound when hitting the ball.

Game 7: The Magician

GOALS

Paying visual attention to another
Practicing winning and losing
Recognizing similarities and differences in others
Maintaining attention in a game
Turn taking

MATERIALS

Three players minimum

SETUP

One person stands in front of the others.

DIRECTIONS

The first person standing in front of the others says, "Look at me." The other players look for a count of ten seconds. Then, instruct the group to close their eyes. The person in front then changes something about her appearance (for example, she unbuttons one button, puts a hand on her hip, moves her hair to the other side, or rolls up a sleeve). When she is ready she says, "Abracadabra, one, two, three . . . What is different about me?" The group then opens their eyes, and anyone who has a guess raises a hand. Pick someone with a hand raised, and if he is correct he gets the next turn to be the "magician."

MODIFICATION

If people are peeking (which is often the case!), the group may have to put their hands over their eyes, bend their heads down, or completely turn around.

Game 8: Hamburger Ball

GOALS

Teamwork
Communication
Proprioceptive and kinesthetic awareness
Gross motor planning
Fine motor planning
Multiple step sequencing

MATERIALS

Materials needed for each two-person team: a larger-size ball (soccer ball, football, beach ball) or an equivalent-size cushion (the hamburger), two T-shirts (the bun), two pairs of rolled-up socks (the pickles), three crumpled pieces of newspaper (the tomatoes), and one small washcloth (the lettuce); a space large enough for players to walk back and forth—at least a twenty-foot distance; a timer or watch; and three persons minimum (or two persons per each additional team)

SETUP

Group each team's items together at one end of the space so that each team of two gets the same items. Determine to where players will walk to build their "hamburger."

DIRECTIONS

Players are going to try to build a hamburger! The two people on each team will position one or more items pressed between their bodies so it doesn't fall down; hook elbows, standing back-to-back; and then walk across the room without letting the object fall out. They go back and forth until all items are brought over, and then they assemble their burger. Players may group ingredients together, for example carrying two T-shirts for the bun or all pairs of socks for the pickles at one time. If a team drops any items, the players need to return to the starting place and begin again. Whichever team builds their hamburger the fastest wins!

MODIFICATIONS

1. If you don't have enough material for all teams to build simultaneously, then each team takes a turn using all the same items, and you time which team builds their burger the fastest.

2. Have the teams reverse themselves and face forward in a hugging position. Please note, however, that this may be too threatening for those children who don't like such close proximity to others.

Game 9: Voice Remote Control

GOALS

Auditory volume awareness (knowing *how* to use a loud or soft voice)
Social awareness (knowing *when* to use different volumes of speech— inside versus outside voice)
Listening
Turn taking
Following directions

MATERIALS

A small rectangular piece of cardboard or posterboard cut to about ten inches wide and four inches tall, a large paper clip, a large marker, a book appropriate to the age group or a song everyone knows (optional), and two players

SETUP

Draw a horizontal line all the way across the center of the ten-inch cardboard strip, halfway between the top and bottom edges. On top of the line write the numbers 1, 2, 3, and 4, evenly spaced about every two inches apart. Attach the paper clip to the bottom of the cardboard strip so you can slide it from left to right along the bottom.

DIRECTIONS

One child will be the speaker, and the other will be the "Voice Remote Controller." The speaker starts reading a book or singing a song (if a song, everyone can practice singing along). Holding the "remote" (the cardboard strip), the Voice Remote Controller faces the person talking. When the Voice Remote Controller says "Stop," he will slide the paper clip to a different number (1 being the softest and 4 being the loudest). The speaker will then adjust her voice volume accordingly.

MODIFICATIONS

1. Children who are not able to read can look at a book and make up the words or tell their own story, or they can sing a song.

2. Go on to practice specific social scenarios in which you would use a soft versus a loud voice. Ask children, "When would you use a low volume 1? Or a high volume 4?" For example, remind them that when you are in a library or someone is trying to sleep, you would use a low volume, but when there is an emergency, like a fire, you want to yell "Fire!" or "Help!" at a high volume.

3. Have them brainstorm scenarios and practice them.

Game 10: The Detective

GOALS

Visual memory recall
Perceptual motor skills
Turn taking
Peer collaboration

MATERIALS

A large, plain-colored towel or blanket, and five to ten miscellaneous objects (toothbrush, key, ball, phone, rubber band, sock . . .), the number depending on the children's ages and capabilities; and three persons minimum

SETUP

Lay the towel (or blanket) flat on the floor and place the objects randomly all over the towel.

DIRECTIONS

One person will be the detective and has to look at all the objects for one minute. She then turns her back, and the others remove one of the objects that they have mutually decided on together. The detective now has to look and identify which object is missing. Have children take turns being the detective.

MODIFICATIONS

1. To modify the challenge, either reduce or increase the number of objects.

2. Try removing two and then three objects at a time.

3. If you have many players, teammates can help give "clues" to the detective ("It starts with the letter _____," or "You use it to _____").

CHAPTER FIVE

Short Group Games for Ages Three to Fifteen

Sometimes you just need a single short game. Maybe you want to empha-size a lesson with a movement component. Maybe you need to get every-one's circulation going to renew their alertness. Maybe you sense that the children have sat long enough and you want to bring in that joy that comes from laughter and action. If those are your needs, these games are for you.

The game could be as simple and joyous and short as in the ending of "Shoe Leaps," in which all children put their shoes in a pile and, one by one, take a running leap over them while the others do a drum roll and shout each person's name as he or she soars through the air.

Or maybe, if the students are studying at shared tables, they take a break when you place a marble on each table. Their mission in "Marble Play" is to keep that marble moving by batting it around to each other without allowing it to fall off—a fun challenge in staying alert and fast reflexes.

Or get a ball, form a circle, and reinforce the day's lesson by tossing the ball to each other while playing "Category Ball Game." Doing history? Whoever catches the ball has to state a cause of the American Revolution. Discussing grammar? The catcher has to say a verb.

Chris and the Box

Chris came into the school's playroom reluctantly. He tends to be reluctant about most activities in which he isn't the initiator. Chris is a child with autism and is especially uncomfortable with anything new. Today's new thing was a huge box sitting in the middle of the rug. Other kids were all around the box. Chris stood by the glass door, looking out and turning his back to us, giving us the message that he would rather be out than in. But the kids began to sing a song and play a game involving the box, and finally curiosity won him over and he watched from a distance as we placed his schoolmate, Kaya, inside the box. We loosely closed the top flaps and crooned,

Who's in the box?
Who's in the box?
Knock knock knock
Who's in the box?

Kaya popped up, and we said, "It's Kaya!" We gave Kaya a couple more turns while Chris watched and even tentatively knocked on the box.

"It's Chris's turn," we said, and he let us put him inside next and immediately sat down, so we closed the flaps. Again we crooned our tune and knocked softly on the box in case the noise would irritate him. To our surprise, he popped up with a huge grin on his face, and we said, "It's Chris!"

Chris liked the game so much that he wanted several turns, and then was in such a good mood that he was willing to play the next game when we turned the box on its side, opened up all the flaps, and had the children crawl through the "tunnel." Because we know that children with autism often respond better to songs than they do to just words, we made up a short, simply song to accompany the game:

Crawl through the tunnel
Crawl through the tunnel
All the way to the end

Like all children, children on the autism spectrum are unique in their interests, and no one game fits all. And yet, many enjoy activities that involve small, safe spaces and even tight enclosures. Being inside a box and crawling through one are fun ways to serve that need!

These games, just like all the others in this book, may seem like just plain fun. But look beneath and you'll see the motor, sensory, and social components that are present. And dare I add the spiritual component? After all, being present in the moment and connected to everyone else has its own soulful rewards.

Short Games for Young Children (Ages Three to Ten)

Game 1: Shoe Leaps

The best thing about this game is that there are always shoes around, so it can easily be played at home or in the classroom.

GOALS

Motor planning (knowing how high or far to jump)
Timing
Balance

Being comfortable with being the center of attention

Awareness of others

Turn taking

MATERIALS

Children's shoes and a large space for running and jumping

SETUP

Have a pile of shoes ready. At first, one shoe at a time will be used, and at the end, they all will be.

DIRECTIONS

The players start by jumping over one shoe; then two in a line, which are placed end-to-end or next to each other depending on how quickly or slowly you want the line to grow (older players want it to get long fast!); then three; and so on until the line of shoes is so long that no one can make it from one end to the other. For the finale, all of the shoes are piled in one place, and the players then have to run and leap over the whole pile!

MODIFICATION

If you want to add an element of social awareness in a group setting, you can ask each child to find someone else's shoes. "Annie, can you find Liam's shoes and bring them to him?" You might find, as I often have, that the children with Down syndrome are often the best at pairing the people with their correct shoes.

Game 2: Blindfold

I recently got upgraded to first class, an unusual event, but one of the less obvious perks was the blindfold they gave us to help us sleep. I knew it would be a good prop for a blindfold game.

GOALS

Experiencing peers on sensory levels

Allowing touch

Being aware of differences in voices, sizes, and physical details (hair
length, height, waist size, and so on)

MATERIALS

A blindfold

SETUP

One child is blindfolded and standing in front of an adult (you might want
to sit on a chair for this).

DIRECTIONS

The blindfolded child has to guess who a person is by feeling him. A friend is quietly brought in front of the
blindfolded child, who uses her hands to determine various qualities based on such
prompts as "Does this person have
long or short hair?" "Is this person taller or shorter than you?"
"Is this person bigger or smaller
than you?" The child then guesses
who that person is.

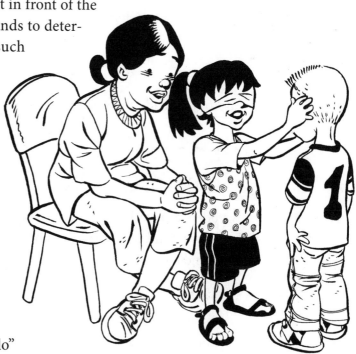

Once the child has made her
guess, you lift the blindfold so she
can see if she was correct. Then, the
person who was felt becomes
the one who is blindfolded and
gets to guess next. If the guesser
is having a hard time, add voice.
Have the person being felt say "Hello"
or a sentence.

MODIFICATIONS

1. In some classes, especially if children seem shy about touching others, I use voice as the only form of identification. Identifying a voice is often easier than feeling.

2. If I don't have a blindfold, I use a paper bag with a friendly face drawn on the front. It allows for a lot of breathing space, but children can look down and see the shoes of the child standing in front of them. That's okay, through—the game can even be changed to "Whose Shoes Are These?"

3. You can add a song or chant to give a time limitation to each person's turn. I sing the words that follow. The tune is from an old Campbell's Soup commercial, but any tune or simply chanting will do.

> Who is this?
> Who is this?
> Can you tell me
> Who is this?

VIDEO

http://gameslady.com/video/single/blindfold.asp

Game 3: Can You Do the Can-Can?

A student at a workshop in Vancouver, Canada, came up with this movement-based eye-hand coordination game that has mathematical possibilities and a lively and familiar tune.

GOALS

Turn taking
Social awareness
Coordination
Working with others

MATERIALS

Enough cans for everyone to have one (if a small group, two or more cans per person)

SETUP

Children sit in a circle with their cans. Cans can be of any kind, such as soft drink cans, food cans, or small cat food cans. The only criteria are that they are clean, there is nothing sharp to cut fingers, and the cans fit nicely on top of each other. If they only fit if stacked one way, that is okay. Children will learn to notice that detail.

DIRECTIONS

One by one, the children add their can to an ever-growing tower of cans. The children are taught a simple song to go with the movements, like this variation on the traditional song to accompany the Can-Can dance:

> Can can can you do the can can
>
> Can you do the can can
>
> Can you do the can can can can can

When the tower of cans inevitably falls over, the children can count the number of cans that fell. If you want to add to the mix, have them combine the number of cans that fell with the number of cans that are still standing.

MODIFICATIONS

1. You aren't limited to towers; you can have the children make a pyramid with the cans instead.
2. You can sing the words slowly or very quickly to change the tempo and the excitement of the players.

VIDEO

http://gameslady.com/video/single/can-can.asp

Game 4: Can You Do What I Do? Can You Say What I Say?

GOALS

Singing in sync with others
Rhythm
Taking turns in a timely fashion

SETUP

The group sits in a circle or in view of each other.

DIRECTIONS

With those two simple lines, you can open up a world of imitation. Children learn by imitating things, whether it is how to pronounce a word or how to do an action. In this circle game, the chant "Can you do what I do? Can you say what I say?" is repeated, and the leader does whatever sound and gesture he wants. The others all imitate that sound and the gesture. The beauty of the game is that there are no wrong sounds to make, no wrong gestures. Anything is okay. Really. For all sounds are, in the end, just sounds.

MODIFICATION

Children who are nonverbal can join in, children whose main language is not yours can sing along. Gestures should be short to fit into the rhythm and can be done or approximated by anyone, whether sitting on the floor or in a wheelchair. This is truly an equal opportunity game.

VIDEO

http://gameslady.com/video/single/can-you-do.asp

Enticing Nona

It all started out so great. Nona saw me walk into her preschool classroom and came right over, knowing that going with me meant going to Social Club, a session I hold twice a month for kids on the spectrum and their friends. Kids like Social Club, in which they will jump on a trampoline, go through an obstacle course, and play many games. I had a homeschooled child with me that day, and Nona took Naj's hand, at my request, to walk her over to the Social Club room.

So far, so good. Nona doesn't usually hold hands. But today Nona was feeling especially happy and became the leader. Naj, also on the spectrum, happily followed her. They were crossing the balance beam, jumping on the squares, climbing down the laddered ramp, and giggling when they were encouraged to jump on the trampoline while holding hands. Their balance challenged by holding hands, they fell, which made them laugh even more along with the shrieks they made when they were tickled as they came out of the tunnel at the end of the obstacle course. I showed the girls how to walk backward on the balance beam while holding on to each other. Nona put her arms around her new friend, and they walked backward on the beam together.

Then it all changed. After many turns around the obstacle course circuit, we introduced the next activity, "Throw at the Pictures," in which children take turns throwing a beanbag at different pictures. The pictures were drawings of common things, such as a yellow sun, a white sailboat, and a red stop sign. We gave instructions that fit each child's cognitive level. "Throw the ball at the sun" (or for the more advanced, "the color yellow" or "the circle"). "Throw the ball at the boat" (or "the color white" or "the triangle"). "Throw the ball at the stop sign" (or "the color red" or "the octagon").

Nona wanted every turn. She knows all the shapes. When others, even Naj, had a turn, Nona's protest took the form of throwing herself on the floor, yelling.

Nona has done this before. It's her MO. As the occupational therapist, I often come into the inclusive classrooms to play a motor game with everyone. Nona wants to play but doesn't get the concept of turn taking. She wants her turn first and every turn after. When she doesn't get it, she might fall to the floor and act as if she fell and hurt herself and moan theatrically (she's good at this!).

At first the reaction to her method got her a lot of reassuring that she was okay, that everything was okay. This reaction encouraged her style of doomed behavior that would not make her any friends. What has proven to work best is to ignore her behavior, go on with life, and let her rejoin the group in her own time.

This day, while she was lying on the floor moaning, the rest of us moved over to the table to play a fast game of "Bat the Box." It's a simple game and can be played with even a tissue box. The box is batted from person to person, sliding easily along the tabletop. The speed of the game encourages focused attention and reacting quickly. It's easy to bat the box, and that keeps the game lively and everyone successful. We add a chant:

> Bat the box and bat the box
> How fast can you doooo it?

By repeating this chant rhythmically, it keeps the children's focus on the box and adds the challenge of speed.

While we were playing this game, Nona stopped wailing, got quiet, and watched. We began the next game, "Find the Creature." This game involves finding the little plastic creatures hidden in a box of sand. We added a spontaneous chant to go along with the action of searching and finding. The chant was accompanied by hand slaps, using the table as our drum. Slapping the table keeps all children involved, even when it's not their turn with the sand box. The chanting is long enough to give players each time to find something and lets them know the beginning and end of their turn.

> What did you find in the sand?
> (slap . . . slap . . . slap-slap-slap)
> In the sand?
> (slap-slap-slap)

In the sand?

(*slap-slap-slap*)

What did you find in the sand?

(*slap . . . slap . . . slap-slap-slap*)

You found a _____!

Pass the sand to your friend

(drum roll as the box is being passed—*slap-slap-slap-slap-slap*)

Nona came over and quietly sat down. We passed her the box, and while we chanted for her, she dug into the sand and found a little plastic gecko. "Pass the sand to your friend," we concluded while pushing the box, our hand over hers, to the next person. "Nona's turn," she said, but her heart wasn't in it. She wanted to stay and play, and maybe she saw that others' turns only lasted the length of a short song.

After all the creatures were found, we changed the game to "Comb the Sand" by adding a comb to the sand box. The new chant was:

> Comb and comb and comb the sand
>
> Comb the sand
>
> Comb the sand
>
> Comb and comb and comb the sand
>
> Pass the sand to your friend

Combing the sand and making a pattern with the teeth of the comb is such a calming activity. It's not surprising that there is a Buddhist practice using sand and a rake.

For the last part of the game, I gave the players tiny cups of water to pour on the sand, making it delightfully crunchy and squeezable and fun to poke at. Nona especially liked poking holes in the wet sand with her finger. She and Naj, buddies again in the end, giggled and poked the sand together.

Game 5: Group Dance

Chorography seems like the domain of expert dancers, but as the African saying goes, "If you can talk, you can sing, and if you can walk, you can dance!" In the same vein, if you can dance, you can choreograph your own dance. And, better yet, a group of people can make up their own dance together and dance it on the spot!

GOALS

Imitating what others are doing

Creating one's own move

Understanding a sequence of movements

Being part of a whole dance

Performing and being in sync

SETUP

The group (of three to six people) stands in a circle.

DIRECTIONS

The first person in the circle makes up any movement he wants. It could be, for example, jumping up and down, or waving his arms, or shaking his booty. Everyone immediately copies that movement. Then the next person does another movement. The group does the first movement followed by the second. Then, the third person adds a third movement, and the group puts all three together in the same order: for example, arms above the head shaking back and forth, followed by hips swaying from side to side four times, followed by foot stomping four times.

Continue this activity until everyone has had a turn to add to the dance. IT IS IMPORTANT THAT EVERYONE PRACTICE THE WHOLE SET FROM BEGINNING TO END EACH TIME A NEW MOVEMENT IS INTRODUCED. If this is done, it is easier for everyone to remember the series. The child who may have difficulty with remembering can easily copy what the others are doing.

MODIFICATIONS

1. Dancing naturally elicits sounds, so feel free to add "do-wahs" or musical tunes to the dance. For example, the shaking of the arms can be accompanied by the sound "boop boop be doop." The hip sway can have the sounds "la la de da." Foot stomping can be "one, two, three, four." You get the idea.

2. The beauty of this game is that everyone can do it. Even a child with special needs has a movement, and you can help the child who is unsure of what's going on by suggesting a movement you know she knows, such as clapping her hands, and encouraging her to copy

the other movements. You may need to stand behind the person and help move her at first until she gets the idea. Imitating others' movements is an important step in learning, and doing it in dance is a delightful way to learn this lesson!

VIDEO

http://gameslady.com/video/single/group-dance.asp

Game 6: Horse Is Walking

When I was younger, I liked to play this vigorous game with kids in which one person was the "Lookout" and the others were members of the tribe. The game would start out with everyone whooping and hollering and dancing and singing. Then suddenly the Lookout would pretend to spy a dangerous leopard and would sit down and be motionless, like a statue. The members of the tribe who were paying attention would immediately sit and freeze as well. The game was about who could go from full movement to stopping and sitting the quickest. Whoever could would be the Lookout next. In a similar way in this game, everyone goes from moving together, sometimes very quickly, to stopping suddenly.

GOALS

Imitating movements
Listening to words to determine movement
Watching what the leader is doing
Being in sync with others
Increasing vocabulary ("trotting," "cantering," and "galloping")

SETUP

Everyone sits around in a circle.

DIRECTIONS

In this game, the "horse" goes from walking to jumping, trotting, cantering, and galloping. But in between, at some point, he stops. And everyone who is playing stops too. Instead of actually running around the room, the players clap their hands against their legs at different speeds to represent the horse's movements. Chant the following as you do the motions, and encourage everyone to join in (the words are easy):

The horse is walking, walking, walking

The horse is walking

(clap legs—right, left, right, left, and so on)

Now he stops

The horse is jumping, jumping, jumping

The horse is jumping

(clap legs—both hands at the same time)

Now he stops

The horse is trotting, trotting, trotting

The horse is trotting

(alternate hands again, but do it faster)

Now he stops

The horse is cantering, cantering, cantering

The horse is cantering

(alternate hands even faster)

Now he stops

The horse is galloping, galloping, galloping

The horse is galloping

(clap both legs with both hands at the same time along with bouncing the body, if desired)

Now he stops!

You can always just make the words predictably rhythmic as well and keep the same beat throughout, rather than vary clapping speeds. It depends on the needs and skills of your group.

MODIFICATION

You can also make the game stimulate children's creativity by asking, "What else can the horse do?" The words of the song and the accompanying gestures change depending on their responses. For example, the horse is swimming, swimming, swimming (eating, running, waving, driving, and so on).

VIDEO

http://gameslady.com/video/single/horse-walking.asp

Game 7: Marble Play

I was sitting at an outside table with a group of elders, most of whom were in wheelchairs and hard of hearing. I was the social director. They had played games with me before, so they weren't surprised when I got the idea of batting the box of Kleenex to the person across from me. She giggled and batted it back. Game on. We batted the box to and fro and back and forth to each person, and everyone was tickled by the silliness of the game. I was pleased because it meant that everyone was focused, interacting, and paying attention to the present moment. What more could a social director want?

Playing the same game using a marble with a group of mixed students produces the same results. Don't fret if the marbles keep falling off the table; the game is about focusing attention and having fun playing with others. It helps to have a few marbles available so that if one drops, time isn't spent looking for it immediately.

GOALS

Watching and being ready to move

Fine motor skills

Awareness of others

Quick reflexes

Focused attention

MATERIALS

A few marbles

SETUP

Players sit around a table.

DIRECTIONS

Roll a marble to a child at one end of the table. She has to catch it and then roll it to someone else. You never know who is going to get the marble next, so it behooves all to pay attention.

MODIFICATION

If things get slow, introduce another marble and maybe even another. The action can be either careful or crazy! Your choice.

VIDEO

http://gameslady.com/video/single/marble.asp

Game 8: Names, Names, We All Have Names

It's said that the sweetest sound in the world is the sound of your own name. It certainly is true that when someone says your name, you feel noticed. In this game, everyone says your name four times, which can feel like music to your ears.

GOALS

Listening to names
Watching what others do
Imitating others' motor gestures and tone

SETUP

The game is usually played in a circle, but can easily be done sitting at desks or in living room chairs.

DIRECTIONS

A chant precedes each person's turn:

> Names, names, we all have names
> You say yours, we'll say the same

If you know sign language or are willing to look up the appropriate gestures in a signing dictionary, it can add a fine motor element to the game. After the chant, the player whose turn it is says his name. In the simplest version of this game, a child says his name—for example, Oliver—and the whole group then claps his name four times, "Oliver, Oliver, Oliver, Oliver." The chant is then repeated for the next person.

MODIFICATION

A more complex response would be to have each child make a different gesture for each syllable. For example:

"O"—hands clap
"li"—arms out in front
"ver"—arms above the head

Another multifaceted response would be to have the children say their name with emotion and gestures. They could say their name with pathos or sadness, with joy and gladness, with fear or surprise, or even with confusion: "Oliver?" or "Oliver!" or "OLIVER" . . .

VIDEO

http://gameslady.com/video/single/name-names.asp

Game 9: Tell Us What You Like to Do

When I was in my twenties I read a book called *Wishcraft* by an author with my name, Barbara Sher. In the book she suggested that one write down twenty things one likes to do and then categorize them. One category would be "Does it cost money, or is it free?" Another would be "Is it something to do alone or with others?" I had thought of myself as very social, so I was surprised to find that the things I enjoyed the most were all solitary experiences, such as writing, playing with clay, doing an art project, taking walks in the woods, and messing around on the piano. Because of that new awareness, I began to schedule those types of activities in my life, whereas before they were catch-as-catch-can occurrences.

And that, as it's said in a Robert Frost poem, "made all the difference."

GOALS

Self-awareness
Awareness of others

SETUP

Children sit in a circle.

DIRECTIONS

During circle time or group time, ask the children to take turns saying what they like to do. You might give them some time to think about it beforehand by announcing earlier that this game will be played later in the day.

Sing the following chant or tune after each person's turn (the tune is an abbreviated version of "Mary Had a Little Lamb").

Tell us what you like to do
Won't you tell us now?

Nikolai Finds Art

Nikolai walked into the room screaming. His beautiful Russian mother had told him that he was going to stay in the classroom without her, and he was not pleased. He had always been with either his mom or his nanny, and even one moment without them was too long. "He showers with me. He sleeps with me. It too much," his mom complained. I was worried about his being there without her for my own reasons. I knew he'd cry loudly, and the loud sounds would affect all the other kids, most of whom were also on the spectrum. Mom left, and a teacher tried to console Nikolai. Nikolai didn't notice. He ran to the window sobbing as if his life was in mortal danger—and from his viewpoint, it was. He had never been on his own, and for all he knew he would not be okay.

The teacher was sympathetic and talked with him about the situation, and took him for a short walk, but nothing distracted Nikolai from his woes. I suggested that Nikolai be placed on the teacher's lap and be in a position to just watch what the others were doing.

What the others were doing at that moment was taking turns on a seesaw. The teeter-totter, as others would call it, was improvised out of a rocker board and a two-by-six-foot board. At first the kids took turns sitting on either side of the board and going up and down. The staff all sang an impromptu "up and down and up and down" song to accompany the movement. A third child, wanting to be part of it all and having a hard time waiting for another turn, was placed in the center of the board to experience the movements. The kids giggled and laughed with the sensations. As they began to grow tired of the repetition, we upped the ante, so to speak, and had, at first, just the child in the middle stand on the board, and then all three players stand on the board. Each child was spotted or held by a staff member so that the kids could enjoy the challenge to their balance without harsh risks.

The children were clearly enjoying themselves, and their joyous sounds captured Nikolai's attention. He watched and got quieter and quieter. When the game was over, the kids were directed to the next activity, which involved putting plastic garbage bags on over their clothes so they could paint. When Nikolai reached for a garbage bag and said "Plastic," we knew we had captured his interest. He joined the others, who were dipping pieces of celery stalks into paints and pressing the stalks onto poster paper that had been placed on the wall. We used potato pieces and bamboo stalks for variation as well as small brushes that fit on children's fingers. Shallow bowls of red, blue, and yellow paints were conveniently placed on the covered floor by the poster paper and within easy reach.

The children were entranced; especially Nikolai. Even another child who had been diagnosed with attention deficit/hyperactivity disorder had no trouble staying with the activity for the entire twenty-minute period.

I remembered the previous time Nikolai attended class with his mother and had only gotten interested in the activity when we had switched to an art project. At that time we were giving the children each a blob of red paint and an ice cube, and their job was to smoosh the blob around with the cold ice cube. The unusualness of messing with an ice cube plus squishing paint kept their interest strong. After a while we'd added a blob of blue color and pointed out how the color turned into purple as the colors mixed together. Later we gave them a fresh piece of paper with yellow paint to smoosh. We eventually added blue to the yellow so they could make green magically appear.

To capture children's attention, it's important to know what interests them. Some people like to do art. Some people love to play in water. Some only respond strongly to movement. Still others prefer activities that require taking things apart and putting them together. Nikolai, we know now, is an "art person." We'll be ready to entice him again with art so that he can continue to experience that life, even without Mommy present, can still be good.

I've found that children tend to have very different responses. For example, in one group, one child liked "to use a telescope and see a shooting star," whereas another one said, "I like to reach up high" (we suspect that in his house the "good things" are put out of reach!).

MODIFICATION
Have children say what they want to do when they are grown-ups.

Game 10: Throw at the Letters

Children enjoy throwing. Little ones may just like the experience of throwing, but as they grow and become increasingly more adept, they prefer aiming. Carnival barkers take advantage of that desire by promising a teddy bear as a reward for the person who can knock the bottles down. Teachers can also take advantage of that desire by making throwing a way to answer questions.

GOALS
Eye-hand coordination
Letter, phonic, or number recognition
Turn taking
Listening to instructions
Watching others

MATERIALS
A chalkboard and chalk, and a beanbag

SETUP
Have all or some of the letters of the alphabet written on the chalkboard. Children can be sitting in a semicircle facing the chalkboard.

DIRECTIONS
Give each child a letter target to throw at, such as "Throw the beanbag at the letter *B*." Have children take turns throwing at different letters.

MODIFICATIONS

1. Besides letter recognition, preschoolers can practice phonics, as in "Throw at the letter that says 'grrr.'" Or use numbers for number recognition or sight words or rhyming words. An older child can throw at multiple numbers (for example, "Throw at the sequence of numbers 7, 6, 4, 5").

2. Even high school students can play this game using content-related questions. For example, if learning the symbols on the periodic table, the prompt might be, "Throw at the symbol for lead." Or this game might be used to reinforce recognition of mathematical symbols.

VIDEO

http://gameslady.com/video/single/throw-at-letter.asp

Game 11: Twist on the Twister

Everyone knows the game Twister. It comes with a plastic sheet imprinted with four lines of colored dots. The game also has a spinner, and the object is to have the players put different body parts on different colored spots and, in a sense, get twisted up together. This can be a fun game, but there is another way to use that plastic sheet of dots that speaks directly to the needs of the developmentally younger child.

GOALS

Body awareness

Balance

Color recognition

Listening to instructions

Identifying colors

Turn taking

Having physical contact with others

MATERIALS

A Twister mat

SETUP

Lay the sheet on the floor.

DIRECTIONS

Ask each child to do a series of actions on the sheet. For example:

1. Stand on the red dot.

2. Jump twice on the next two red dots.

3. Jump sideways to the yellow dot.

4. Jump backward to the yellow dot behind you.

5. Hop forward on one foot on each green dot.

6. Jump all the way to the last green dot.

MODIFICATIONS

1. Each child can make up directions for others to follow.

2. A group can all play together. For example: there are five red dots, so you could have five children stand on each red dot. Then ask them all to keep one foot on the red dot and put their other foot on the yellow dot in the next row. Then have them put both hands on the green dot in the next row, and finally their nose on the blue dot in the last row!

VIDEO

http://gameslady.com/video/single/twister.asp

Short Games for Older Kids (Ages Seven to Fifteen)

- - - ‿ - ‿ - ‿ - ‿ - ‿ - ‿ - ‿ - ‿ - ‿ - ‿ - ‿ -

Game 1: Bowling for Dollars

Soft drink aluminum cans are ubiquitous. It's easy to collect ten of them to provide a game that gives children a fun and friendly, competitive way to practice mentally computing various combinations of coins.

This game is for children seven years old and older. Even adults enjoy it and say it's like being on a game show.

GOALS

Estimating
Eye-hand coordination
Working as a team
Math

MATERIALS

Ten empty aluminum cans; the following coins: one half dollar, two quarters, three dimes, two nickels, and two pennies (or pictures or names of these coins); a ball or beanbag; colored paper (optional); and a pen and paper (optional)

SETUP

To prepare for the game, tape a coin (or a picture or name of a coin) to the bottom of each can.

DIRECTIONS

The cans are set up in a horizontal row facing the players, and each player gets a turn to knock down a can with a ball (or a beanbag). After each can is knocked down, the value of the coin on the bottom of the can is written down, if the players can't remember the total number. The object is to knock down as many cans as necessary to get coins whose values add up to a dollar BUT do not exceed that amount.

Separate the cans enough so that the ball will not knock over more than one can at a time.

Divide the class into teams. The first team begins with one of its members knocking down a can. Then the next member knocks down a can. The amounts on the bottom of the can are added together, and the team decides if they can knock down another can without the final amount going over a dollar. If they go over a dollar, they automatically lose. Each team gets a turn to bowl. The team that stays under a dollar but has the highest amount wins. If the cans are different colors, children will begin to memorize which cans have which coins on the bottom. If you don't have similar cans and don't want memory to be a factor, cover the cans with paper of the same color.

This game involves teamwork and can easily be played with a mixed-skill-level team so all children are part of the game. Besides practicing computing skills, children get experience in working as a team to estimate and make group decisions. In addition, they are getting a chance to work on their eye-hand coordination!

VARIATION

Feel free to make your own variations on the game and use more or fewer cans and different combinations of coins. For example, the goal can be any amount: $5.00, $7.10, whatever!

MODIFICATIONS

1. You can modify this game for children with special needs. The child with special needs can . . .

   ◆ Get closer to the cans when throwing

   ◆ Be in charge of adding the amounts

   ◆ Be in charge of resetting the cans for the next team after they are knocked down

   ◆ Be in charge of retrieving the ball and tossing it to the next player

2. For younger children, instead of a computing game, make it a simple adding game. Have class members each bowl down as many cans as they can and then add up the amount knocked down.

Game 2: Category Ball Game

Here is a simple ball game that can reinforce cognitive skills.

GOALS

Cognitive memory
Public performance
Focusing
Auditory awareness
Social awareness

MATERIALS

A large ball (or one made of bunched-up newspapers taped together)

SETUP

Children stand in a circle with the large ball, with one child or adult holding the ball. The larger the ball, the easier it is to catch, which reduces the chance of a child's being embarrassed by missing the catch and allows players to focus instead on coming up with an answer.

DIRECTIONS

One person names a category, such as "names of flowers," and throws the ball to another person. The person who catches the ball has to name a type of flower, such as "daisy." Then the ball is thrown to the next person, who has to come up with the name of another flower. Players can throw the ball to anyone in the circle or to the person who is standing next to them.

The game continues until someone cannot think of an answer, and that gives the person the right to come up with another category, such as "forms of transportation." The person would then say one form, such as "car," before throwing the ball. The person catching it would say another form, such as "train," and so one. Categories can change anytime anyone who has the ball would like to start a new category.

One of the best parts of this game is the built-in "no-fail" element. If a person can't think of an answer, she is allowed to change the category. Thinking of a new category still keeps her brain moving and in the cognitive game!

MODIFICATIONS

1. Category themes could be aimed at the elementary level, such as names of animals, forms of transportation, counties, continents, colors, or names of people in the class.

2. Categories can be elevated for the high school level by using such subjects as symbols of the periodic table, painters of the Renaissance period, writers of autobiographical fiction, and so on.

Game 3: Compliment Me

I doubt that we really would ever tire of hearing good things said about us, if done sincerely. In this game, it's possible to hear good things and to say them anonymously.

GOALS

Awareness of others' strengths
Compassion and kindness to others
Self-awareness

MATERIALS

Paper and pens

SETUP

Type up a list of the people in the group and a list of complimentary descriptive words on two separate sheets. Some examples of descriptions are kind, patient, understanding, open minded, cheerful, optimistic, cute, lovely, loving, warm, loyal, thoughtful, generous, honest, wise, gentle, fair, funny, handsome, polite, respectful, sweet, silly, compassionate, sympathetic, intelligent, hard worker, peaceful, assertive, cooperative, beautiful, good athlete, dancer, artist, musician, careful, intelligent, charming, forceful, sensitive, good company, helpful, witty, and good sense of humor.

Make enough copies of each sheet for everyone in the group to have two sheets.

DIRECTIONS

Children each write their own list with a descriptive, complimentary word next to each person's name. Or pass the list of names and the list of descriptive words around the room. Each person has to add a complimentary descriptive word to each person's name.

VARIATIONS

1. When all children have added all of their comments, someone reads each of the descriptions, and the others have to guess who is being described. The good part is that even if they are wrong, the ones whose names were guessed will feel good!

2. Compile the descriptions and give them to each player to take home so that people can keep and treasure the lists of words written about them.

Game 4: Expressing Self with Body

Understanding that our words only tell part of the picture of what we mean, we look at body language and facial expression and tone of voice. In this game, children become aware of how to do this themselves and what to look for in others.

GOALS

Self-awareness
Understanding of feelings
Motor control
Public performance
Reading facial cues and body language
Imagination and creativity

SETUP

Children can be seated at their desk and called up one at a time, or they can be loosely walking around a room trying out some of these suggestions all together.

DIRECTIONS

Ask children to express themselves in these ways:

1. Say with your body: "Yes, no, why, stop, wow, help, go away, you make me sick, I want you, don't leave me, I don't understand, I hate you, I love you, you are nice."

2. Act like: an old, dignified woman; a bag lady; a young girl; a young boy; a baby; a toddler learning to walk; Santa Claus; a coal miner; a very fat man; the Devil.

3. Say with your face (faces have feelings): hungry, mad, scared, lazy, bored, picked on, gloomy, cool, motherly, goofy, proud, guilty, disgusted, anxious, weird, ashamed, joyful, suspicious, cynical.

To Touch and Be Touched

When I first met "Sam," whose name was spelled Psalm, I could see why his parents gave him a biblical name. He is angelic looking: he has a bowl haircut, and his big brown eyes beneath the long brown bangs give him an adorableness that can take your breath away.

He also has another side. With the most devilish grin, he would slyly push another child or bang into her as she innocently walked by him. When she protested or complained to the teacher, Sammy would put on his "Aren't I just adorable?" face, and go back to his solitary play.

Sammy mainly played alone and was nonverbal. Being on the spectrum, he had the classic characteristic of having minimal social skills. He may have wanted to connect with others, but so far all he had figured out was how to physically connect by pushing and banging into them. The teachers and I understood his motivation and explained to him about "soft hands" and how to touch his classmates in more accepting ways. Even the other kids were let in on why Sammy was rough. Both those methods helped.

When I worked one-on-one with Sammy, I knew that if I wanted him to pay attention, it was wise for me to throw a leg over his when we were sitting on the floor or in some way make sure our bodies were touching.

I also contributed to his need to touch and be touched by others with some strong proprioceptive group games. One of these games, "People Sandwich," is one I've played many times. In this game the children stand in a circle. I announce that I'm going to make a sandwich, and I pick one child to stand in the center of the circle and be the bread. Then I ask, "What else shall we put in this sandwich?" The first time we played, I made some suggestions. "Let's add some cheese," I said, and then picked Sammy to be the cheese and put him directly in front of the child who was the bread. It didn't take long for the children to come up with other sandwich ingredients, such as ham, pickles, and tomatoes. Actually, children come up with a lot of ideas for ideal sandwich stuff, such as chocolate, cookies, and even rice. Whatever they say is fine with me, and the child that offered the suggestion symbolizes that specific component and is placed in front of the child just added to the sandwich. I end it with the last child being the piece of bread that makes all the children into a sandwich.

The part that Sammy loves is what happens next. I reach out and squeeze all the kids together and pretend to eat them. The others in the class join me in the pretend, and the room is filled with squiggles and giggles. For Sammy, he gets to feel that deep proprioceptive touch, and, most important, he gets to feel very much a part of the group.

Another game that serves the same purpose is done with a piece of cloth. I start it off by wrapping one child tightly in the cloth and asking her to walk from the starting spot to the ending spot ten feet away. When she reaches that spot, I ask or help her to turn around and jump back to the original spot.

Once every child has a turn and gets the idea, I do what especially pleases Sammy and all the others by wrapping two people together. Together, they perform the same movements. First they walk to the designated spot, and then they turn around and jump together back to the original spot.

I have also wrapped up four children and had them jump together. It was their idea, as almost all children want to be physically connected to others. Think how quickly many kids get into wrestling one another. Although one time when five children were wrapped together and jumping it ended with the children falling and landing all over each other, no one was even a little bit hurt, and the children loved it. But school principals and insurance companies would have freaked if they saw that happen, and I'm not suggesting you do this version. But kids like Sammy . . . they would be in a state of bliss.

MODIFICATION

Children can present their versions of expressions or actions or characters to the class, and the others have to guess what emotion or person or word they are expressing.

Game 5: Interviewing

One of the ways we can know about others is by asking questions. It may be safe to say that everyone's favorite topic is him- or herself, so having others ask you about yourself can be a good thing. It can also be a formal thing.

GOALS

Self-awareness
Awareness of differences
Asking good questions
Listening to answers
Public performance

MATERIALS

A piece of paper and pencil for each person

SETUP

Divide the class into partners.

DIRECTIONS

Ask the players to interview each other and write down their answers. Later they can use these answers to introduce their friend to the class.

Here are possible questions to ask:

- What is your favorite food?
- What is your favorite place to sit in your house?
- Where do you like to go in town?

- Which household chore do you prefer? Which do you detest?
- If you won the lottery, what is the first thing you'd buy?
- What thing makes you the happiest?
- Whom do you most admire?
- What is something you like to do every day or as often as you can?
- Name a place you'd like to live if you had to move.
- Name a job you'd like to do if you could do any job in the world.

Game 6: It's All in the Tone

Words can have vastly different meanings depending on what tone is used and where the emphasis is. We can help children—especially those on the spectrum, who tend to have difficulty noticing the more subtle distinctions—by exaggerating those distinctions and saying the same words in different ways to give them different meanings.

GOALS

Social awareness
Reading facial and body cues
Visual awareness
Auditory awareness
Public performance

SETUP

Five children stand up and face the others who are sitting. Children can take turns being the ones in front.

DIRECTIONS

Assign each of the five players a different emotion: sad, mad, surprised, scared, and confused. You could also add more subtle emotions, such as slightly bored, becoming frustrated, and mildly irritated.

Give all the players the same simple expression, such as "I'm going home." Then have the players each take a turn saying those words with their assigned emotion. Some players may need ideas for how to say the words differently.

MODIFICATIONS

1. If the players are older, you might include the element of romantic or sexy.

2. There are any number of words or sentences to use. Have the players make up some of their own to fit the group.

Game 7: Jumping Math

Sitting and writing the answers to math problems on a worksheet can get old and boring. There has to be a more lively way—and there is, with this game.

GOALS

Auditory awareness
Math
Social participation
Eye-foot coordination
Motor control

MATERIALS

Ten pieces of paper and tape

SETUP

Write the numerals 0 through 9 on the pieces of paper and tape them to the floor in a circle pattern. A circle pattern is easiest, as the player can stand in the middle of the circle and have equal access to any number.

DIRECTIONS

Give players math questions and have them jump to the answers. Here are a few possibilities:

JUMP ON THE NUMBERS THAT ARE THE ANSWER TO 200 X 5.

- ◆ Jump to the single- or double-digit number named, such as 8 or 18.

- ◆ Jump to a multiple-digit number named in the correct order, such as the numbers that make up 30,457.

- ◆ Jump to the answer of an addition problem, such as 2 plus 5.

- ◆ Jump to the answer of a multiplication table question, such as 4 times 4.

- ◆ Jump to the answer of a division problem, such as 16 divided by 4.

- ◆ Jump to the number expressed by the Roman numeral XVI.

MODIFICATIONS

1. This, like all games, can be modified by having a buddy. There is a well-known TV show in which the contestants were allowed to call a friend to help them with the answer. Why not have the same system in a classroom? A buddy can supply the answer by writing it down and having her friend jump to it, as well as by whispering the answer in her friend's ear or jumping with him.

2. I find that sometimes children on the spectrum are likely to know the answers to questions, especially ones involving letter and number

recognition, before many of their classmates. Having such a child be the "resident smarty" who gives help to the others can shine a nice light on that child's skills and raise esteem.

Game 8: Make Up a Handshake

We've come a long way from the high five and the fist bump. There are many ways to do what used to be known as a "handshake."

GOALS

Creativity with a partner
Public performance
Motor control and coordination
Learning by imitating others

SETUP

Players take partners.

DIRECTIONS

Each pair makes up a series of original moves that can be a form of greeting. They practice these moves so that they can smoothly teach them to others. The whole group then gets a turn trying out each pair's moves.

Game 9: Make Up a Story

Writing a creative story can be a challenging assignment. It's so much easier if others are making it up with you.

GOALS

Creativity
Trying out one's spontaneity

Imagination
Understanding story building
Social participation

SETUP

Players sit in a circle or in a line so it is clear whose turn is next.

DIRECTIONS

One person starts a story with one line, and each person takes a turn adding one line. For example:

> There was a wicked witch
>
> Who liked to eat salami
>
> But she ran out
>
> So she called up the seven dwarfs
>
> But they were too sleepy, dopey, and grumpy to come
>
> So she went out to find Spider-Man
>
> "Yoo-hoo, Spider-Man," she called . . .

. . . And so on. The story can get ridiculous, but because there is no wrong or right line, everyone can be comfortably included.

MODIFICATION

Someone can write the whole story down and read the final version aloud.

Game 10: Reflection

Imitation may be the sincerest form of flattery, or maybe it just feels like that when everyone in the room does exactly what you do.

GOALS

Visual awareness
Awareness of details
Rhythm
Imitation
Public performance
Creativity
Social awareness

SETUP

One person stands in front of the others.

DIRECTIONS

The person standing in front of the other children moves, and the others exactly mirror that person's movements as if they were mirror reflections.

MODIFICATION

You can add music of various kinds to get different results.

Game 11: Say a Line

It's good to give children a movement break during the school day, but teachers can be reluctant to lose this learning time. In this game, reviewing what is learned can happen with movement.

GOALS

Cognitive memory
Public performance
Social awareness

SETUP

Players stand in a circle.

DIRECTIONS

Players volunteer to go into the center of the circle one at a time and give an example from a theme that has been named. For example, if the theme is famous quotes, a student would go into the center of the circle and say, "To be or not to be, that is the question." Here are some other possible themes:

- *English*: Quote a line of poetry or name an author or a book from a certain period.
- *History*: Name all the amendments in the Bill of Rights or all the causes of the American Revolution.
- *Science*: Name a scientific theory or one of the planets.
- *Film*: Say a famous line from a movie.

There doesn't need to be a particular sequence or order. Anyone can take one or more turns when the space in the center is empty.

MODIFICATION

Students could mime instead of speaking, and the others have to guess what is being physically expressed.

Game 12: Jail

How do you get out of a jam? In this game, different methods are honored, as players try "whatever works."

GOALS

Social awareness
Learning differences in personalities
Trying different tactics and motor methods

SETUP

Players stand in a circle holding hands or holding each other's waists to form a jail. One player stands inside.

DIRECTIONS

The person inside the circle tries to get out. How to do it? Use force? Use calculated force (pick the weakest link)? Flirt? Negotiate? Sneak under? Afterward, have the group discuss which methods were used and how different ones can work in different circumstances.

Game 13: Shower Curtain Spelling

There are so many ways to play this game with different skill levels or age groups. All it requires is a cheap shower curtain. The goal can be as easy as practicing letter recognition or as complex as spelling, rhyming, or unscrambling letters to make words.

GOALS

Letter recognition
Phonics
Spelling
Rhyming
Learning word families

Eye-hand coordination

Focusing

Social awareness

MATERIALS

A plain shower curtain, a permanent marker, and tape (optional)

SETUP

Lay out a plain plastic shower curtain and write the letters of the alphabet on it from A to Z with a permanent marker. Write them large so that they fill up the whole curtain. Lay the curtain on the floor. Tape down the edges if it seems likely to slip around.

DIRECTIONS

Here are some game variations, starting with the easiest:

- *Letter Recognition*: A player is asked to stand on the letter named and jump to other letters named. For example, "Stand on the letter *H*. Jump forward to the *I*, jump sideways to the *J*, jump backward to the *G*, hop on one foot to the letter *M*, and now do a giant broad jump to the letter *S*."

- *Phonics*: A player has to go stand on the letter that is the first sound of the word. For example, "Go stand on the letter that makes the sound of 'Ta' for 'tiger.'"

- *Spelling*: The player has to jump to the letters that spell a word. It can be any word the player chooses. The others have to say the word spelled. Or it could be a word in a specific category, such as names of animals, forms of transportation, counties, continents, colors, or names of people in the class.

- *Rhyming*: The player has to jump to the letters that spell out a rhyming word. For example, "Jump to the letters of a word that rhymes with 'cat.'"

- *Remembering*: Someone in the class calls out the letters that the student has to jump on. After jumping on the named letters, the student has to say the word that was spelled.

- *The Anagram*: The same as the previous game, except the letters of the words are given in a scrambled order. For example, 'SHOW' might be given in this order: 'WSOH.' The student has to visualize the letters, put them in the right order, and say the word aloud.

- *Twister Play*: Tell a child to put his right foot on one letter, his left on another, his right hand on another, and his left hand on another. More than one child can play at the same time in this game, causing intersecting body parts and a lot of laughter.

MODIFICATIONS

The games can be modified for a motorically or cognitively challenged child by letting her . . .

- Use a beanbag to throw on the letters instead of jumping
- Be the one in charge of calling out the letters
- Be the one who selects which word is used from a list of words
- Guess the word spelled by being shown two or three possible written choices

Game 14: Time Line Game

It can be difficult to remember the order in which events in history occurred. This game makes it easier and fun to do so.

GOALS

Memory
Recalling facts
Social negotiating

MATERIALS

Index cards and a pen

SETUP

Make index cards with the different periods of history written on each one—Renaissance, industrial age, Iron Age, and so on.

DIRECTIONS

Each person holds an index card with a period of history on it, and the players have to put themselves in a line in the correct chronological order. This will lead to a lot of discussion among the players as to who stands where!

MODIFICATION

This game can be made much simpler by having children put themselves in a line from the oldest to the youngest.

Game 15: What's My Line?

There was a television program in my youth in which a panel had to guess the occupation of a guest. They had to figure out whether the guest, for example, was an aeronautical engineer or the person who fed the elephants at the zoo by asking questions that can only be answered by a yes or no.

GOALS

Auditory awareness
Memory
Combining facts
Competition
Working with a group

MATERIALS

Index cards and a pen

SETUP

Make up cards with the names of famous people in any category you want—authors, scientists, historians, and so on—or just in one specific field or time period.

DIRECTIONS

One student holds the card with the name on it, and the others have to figure out who this is by asking questions. There could be a limit to the number of questions. There could also be two or more teams trying to figure it out.

Ignoring Clarissa

Clarissa wore a tutu to school every day, and she had to have her shirt tucked into the tutu just right or she'd scream. She rarely spoke. She often screamed. Her meltdown began the moment it was time to pull up her panties after a pee. We knew it was her tactile sensitivity and respectfully accommodated her need to have her shirt neatly tucked inside the elastic band of the tutu. But sometimes we couldn't do it fast enough.

There were other times when she'd meet with some other seemingly minor frustration, and she would freak. And once she got upset, she didn't know how to find her balance again. Holding her, soothing her, distracting her . . . nothing seemed to help. She'd run to the door and try to dash outside. We'd lock the door, and she would scream. She'd strip off her clothes and run around nude. We'd re-dress her. She'd scream.

Everyone was worn to a frazzle trying to figure out what was the antecedent. Why such an overreaction? Did this screaming method work at home? We found out from her father that it did. Clarissa is on the spectrum, and so is her older sister. Clarissa was considered to be the one "less involved." To keep the peace, screams were accommodated.

We decided to try a different approach. We were going to stop resisting and start ignoring the behavior we wanted gone. She wanted out; we'd open the back door to the enclosed playground and let her out. She would come back on her own. She took her clothes off; they stayed off until she put them back on. She eventually did.

She'd cry loudly or scream. We acted as if it were a distant, unimportant sound.

HOWEVER, when she joined in the games, the circles, or playtime, or did tasks on her own, she was praised lavishly and given lots of delicious attention. It wasn't hard. Clarissa is good at so many things. She's bright and a fast learner on the computer. Clarissa knows phonics, sight words, the names of all her classmates, and how to play the games. Inside her was a little girl who liked to play.

One day in the midst of our "Ignoring Clarissa" strategy, an administrator came to observe the class. She watched quizzically as we ignored this loudly crying child while playing a frolicking game of London Bridge with everyone else. But we knew, from experience, that Clarissa would be irresistibly drawn into participating, and she was.

Clarissa eventually completely gave up screaming for playing. She started wearing other clothes to school. She, on her own, greets her teachers with hugs and eye contact. She still doesn't speak much, but she babbles in a convincing way and communicates her intentions. Clarissa still clearly has autism, but now she's learned something about this life: some ways work and some ways don't, and it's good to have the wisdom to know the difference.

Home Therapy

Karen Beardsley

As a therapist who does home visits, I feel that I have been offered an honored privilege and gift to be invited into a family's home. I have been providing occupational therapy home visits with families around the world for over twenty-five years. My personal goals are twofold: first and foremost, I have my plan for what skills I want to help the child achieve, be they sensory, motor, visual perceptual, cognitive, or social. Second, but just as important, I want to facilitate a *connection*, not just between me and the child but also between the child and his parent or caregiver. I seek to support and empower parents or caregivers with the knowledge and confidence that they too can do this, and to let them know that simply playing games with their child can be a rich learning opportunity. Home therapy has become the most challenging, gratifying, and personally successful part of my practice. It is an intimate and unique opportunity for teaching and learning, not only for families but for therapists as well.

Some parents may find home visits intimidating, unpredictable, or even threatening, whereas others may love and welcome them. Some families may feel like their personal space has been invaded or that they perhaps are being judged on *where* they live, *how* they behave, or even the *way* they are parenting their child. The therapist may also feel intimidated. There have been days when I felt like I was under a magnifying glass, being scrutinized and evaluated by the entire family. There have also been times when I've silently prayed before a visit, *I hope this kid doesn't hide and lock himself in his room again*, or thought,

What if the dog attacks me? Despite these real and valid concerns, home therapy has the potential to be one of the best opportunities for sharing, learning, and sustainability for the child, in large part due to the practical nature of using what the family has and what the child is already familiar with in the home.

What makes home therapy different from therapy in school or clinical settings?

The majority of children spend most of their waking hours each week at home with their family or primary caregiver. So the home is their natural environment, and probably the place with which they are most familiar and where they feel most comfortable. The home therapist becomes the facilitator to engage the child, the child's family, and often the child's friends. I have even invited the family dog on one occasion to be a part of a session in a pool! Children are apt to warm up more quickly to outsiders by being in their own space and often feel more confident taking the lead in expressing the activity they would like. When children lead from their interest, it is a lovely and productive invitation to follow.

What are some of the benefits of home therapy?

I once had a parent say to me after working with her child at home, "Oh! . . . I can do this!!" When parents and caregivers observe therapy sessions and try the strategies and games themselves, it is very empowering. They can do this! Knowing that therapy is very doable in one's life demystifies the "magic" that happens behind closed doors in a therapy clinic.

There are also practical and cost-effective benefits. As economic challenges, budget cuts, insurance quotas, and time constraints grow, it's comforting to know that you can still make do with what you've already got around the house. I often bring in a few select items that I like to work with, but if I mainly use what's there in the home, it becomes more likely that the family will use those items when I'm not around. Mom or Dad can easily grab the leftover newspaper or a blanket or a child's ball and play a fun game with that. Likewise, the child may remember a game or activity the therapist did with his stack of blocks or the laundry basket or a favorite stuffed animal and recreate that game himself. These all become therapeutic learning opportunities that fit comfortably into family members' daily lives.

Practice makes progress.

When children and their families have fun learning new activities, they are likely to play them over and over, such that a one-time-a-week home visit has the potential to turn into two- or three-times-a-week or even daily practice. One father once told me that his son "loved the balloon toss game so much that when we went on holiday Tyler taught it to his grandpa to play with him." I have had classroom teachers tell me about games that I did at home with students that were then shared at recess. I have often observed a "turning point" in the home therapy relationship indicated by a natural transference and carryover of the skills into other areas of a child's life. Children start to engage their siblings or neighbors, and find new ways to interact and play or socialize. Many of the games live on when we don't even know it. It is this repetition that will continue to support the growth of and development of skills in the child over time.

Not long ago I went on a regular morning home visit to work with two boys. One boy, Viktor, brought along his younger cousin who was visiting from Russia. He clearly was planning to join us, and I clearly wasn't expecting him. He did not speak a word of English. Viktor said to me matter-of-factly, "He's my cousin. He will play with us today." And so it was, with the added bonus of practice socially integrating with others. Not only did Viktor get to show off and teach some of the games we play but also he got to be the translator! He had a special role that day, and it was a lovely boost for his confidence and self-esteem. Over and over I have seen children teach and show their peers what to do or how to play a certain game. And we know that one of the best ways to really learn something or integrate a skill is to practice it and teach it to someone else. It may not always turn out the way you planned or wanted, but there lies the opportunity for relationship building and creativity. And for some children who may be on the autism spectrum and need to work on social skills, what better place to practice than in their natural day-to-day environment?

Is play work?

Having two children of my own, I sometimes find myself in that dreaded zone: "Oh, they have a three-week holiday from school, what are we going to do?" One morning my daughter Raina woke up and asked me, "What are we going to do today?" As I lay there pensively, she finally blurted out, "Let's just play today!" and then skipped off. It seemed to her a better response than anything I would have come up with. Playing can seem like a chore for some adults. How often have we found ourselves saying, "Not now," or "I'm too tired." Parents seem to be spending less time with their children these days. We continue to outsource them into so many extracurricular activities. Children often seem overscheduled with "organized" groups and clubs and programs to "enrich" them. We somehow think more is better.

We are all born instinctively knowing how to play. As we get older we somehow lose that momentum and seem to need a "permission slip" of sorts or a reminder to play. But playing **is** the occupation of children. We sometimes forget how it can greatly benefit them, and us, in our fast-paced, multitasking culture. It is my deepest wish that parents will learn how to engage their child at home in new and playful ways—and gain confidence in doing so.

I live in the land of smiles.

I have lived and worked in Thailand for many years. The Thai people have taught me to look at and approach life differently. The local people are endlessly gracious, in the moment, full of heart, and playful. There is a widely used word here, "*Sanuk*," which in Thai means *fun*. If you go anywhere, do anything, spend time with anyone, you will usually be asked, "*Sanuk mai?*" or "*Sabaii jai mai?*" which basically translate, respectively, as "Did you have fun?" or "Is your heart happy?" They remind me constantly not to take life so seriously, to enjoy every moment, and that playing is good for my heart.

Tips for Therapists: How to Organize Your Home Visits

1. **Be on time.** Parents are busy people, as are you, and they are waiting for your visit.

2. **Be flexible.** Go in with a plan and be ready to change it.

3. **Go visual.** One thing I have found helpful is to have a chalkboard to write and draw on or some way to make a visual schedule. For example, in my hour-long home visit I may list three or four activities to accomplish. I always start with a fun, easy movement game; then tend to put the harder, more challenging work in the middle; and usually end by letting the child choose a game. We write or draw it all on our list at the beginning of each session and check our schedule.

4. **Be patient.** Offer choices within your choices. If I want to do a ball game, I might say, "Do you want the bowling game or target toss game?" The reality is, as with any therapy, that you are trying to get children to work on things that are hard for them. Sometimes they just want to play their own games or have a snack or show you their toys. I find children tend to take more liberties when having therapy in their own home than they do elsewhere. There are often more distractions, and you need to learn how to set boundaries and expectations with them.

5. **Be mindful of timing.** Allow yourself time to transition in and out of the home. Arrive early to allow yourself setup time. Likewise, know that after the session is often a time to check in with parents, perhaps write a few notes, or review the plan for the next visit.

6. **Follow up.** I personally like to give families a little "homework," even if it is as simple as trying one small technique or game. It hands some responsibility over to the family and helps reinforce what you are teaching. You can say, "Let's check in next week to see how it goes." Not every parent will comply, but it is a good place to start.

7. **Remember that YOU are the therapist.** Lastly, be careful not to overwhelm families with your list of suggestions for what they can do or try. You are there as their child's therapist, and hopefully they trust that you are the doing the job that they are unable to.

Tips for Parents: How Can You Collaborate with Home Therapists?

1. **Be there.** Therapists are busy people, as are you, and they are taking the time to travel there to see your child.

2. **Observe.** Some parents may enjoy being involved with a home visit the entire time, whereas others may feel relief to turn it all over to the therapist. It is not necessary that you stay for an entire session, but take a peek now and then to see what the therapist is doing. You can also join in or take the lead now and then. Seeing your child perk up in response to your playing with him will be thrilling and give you the confidence to do this or other games on other days.

3. **Follow your child's lead.** Look for what your child is engaged in and follow that. Children learn when they are engaged. They will guide you to games that you can build on. It's often easy to go in with our own agenda, but try asking them what they want to play. It's about making a connection first.

4. **Start slow and keep it positive.** Just start with one game at a time. Ask your child for ideas about how to change or adapt the game. If it is not fun the way you are playing it, your child will often know how to make it fun! Kids are great at coming up with new ways to do things.

5. **Don't overwhelm yourself or your child.** If you are really organized, you can make index cards listing individual games and group them by categories. Have your child pick a card from different categories to play a game. You can also toss the cards in a basket and have him randomly choose one. It makes it more of a fun surprise this way. The two of you can determine how many cards and how often.

6. **Remember that YOU are the parent or caregiver.** Remember, you do not have to be your child's therapist. Any games or activities you play with your child are a bonus, and all help support his development and your relationship with him. Keep it light. If it's not fun, it often isn't therapeutic.

About the Authors

Barbara Sher, MA, OTR, has over forty years experience as a pediatric occupational therapist. She is the author of nine books on games, which have been published in eight languages, including Danish, Estonian, Chinese, Russian, and Italian. Her books feature games to elevate attention span, self-esteem, academics, motor skills, and social awareness, and always to promote delightful learning moments for all kids. Her most recent previous book is *Early Intervention Games: Fun, Joyful Ways to Develop Social and Motor Skills in Children with Autism Spectrum or Sensory Processing Disorders.*

She has also given workshops on making inclusive games and learning toys out of easy-to-find materials in many countries, including Cambodia, New Zealand, England, Vietnam, Norway, Nicaragua, Hong Kong, Honduras, and the islands of Micronesia.

Information on her books and more can be found at her Web site, http://gameslady.com, and the books are available through online bookstores.

Karen Beardsley, OTR, has been a pediatric occupational therapist specializing in early childhood for over twenty-five years. She has worked extensively with children who have sensory processing, neuromuscular, and feeding disorders in clinics, schools, and homes. She has ten years of international work experience developing school-based programs in the Pacific Islands and was instrumental in establishing a rehabilitation center and school for refugee children with special needs in Thailand. She has taught workshops in the United States and Asia. Karen currently lives with her husband and two daughters in Phuket, Thailand, where she has a private practice and works collaboratively with families and schools.

Index - - ~ - ~ - ~ - ~ - ~ - ~ - ~ - ~ - ~ - ~ - ~ - .